Keto Diet Cookbook for Beginners:

Achieve Your Weight Goals with a L[...] [...]ed to Revitalize Your Metabolism [II ED[...]

Copyright © 2023
Sarah Roslin

TABLE OF CONTENTS

1 INTRODUCTION

The Keto or the Ketogenic Diet as it should be known in full may seem to be a relatively new diet, but it is not. The Ketogenic Diet has originally been used in the 1920s to alleviate the instances of seizures in epileptic patients. From this initial application in the alleviation of neurological disorders, the Keto Diet as it is now popularly called, has now been part of a trend promoted by celebrities and dietitians as an effective way for people to lose weight.

As you read this book, you may have weight loss as your main objective to go on the Keto Diet, but its advantages are far more extensive as it not only helps you lose weight, but also assist in the effective control of glucose and in the reduction of the growth of tumors among other benefits that are to be discussed later. By this time, your interest in the Keto diet has been effectively piqued, so we go now to the basis on how this diet actually works in your body.

1.1 The Physiology of Ketogenesis

Our body utilizes glucose as the primary energy source to ensure that the cells in the body are able to effectively function. Glucose is obtained as a byproduct of the breakdown of carbohydrates in our body, and is more often easily obtained from simple sugars and starches. However, when we consume excessive levels of glucose that the body does not need to metabolize, the body stores these glucose molecules in the liver in the form of glycogen. The body also begins to store excess glucose within the adipose cells of the body, which leads to the accumulation of fat.

The key with the application of the Keto Diet is that one has to forego the consumption of carbohydrates as the main energy source of the body, and cause the body to undergo Ketogenesis. When the body finds that it is unable to utilize enough glycogen and other carbohydrate stores in the body, it begins to break down the fat cells to release the glucose stored within the fat. When fat is metabolized by the body, it releases the stored glucose, in greater amounts compared to that of carbohydrate sources. It also has the effect of the release of ketones, a byproduct of fat metabolism, and for which this diet is named. You will notice if your body has started Ketogenesis if your breath happens to smell fruity, although you will need to be careful on how you go about with the diet.

While this diet is effective for weight loss and for the effective use of glucose, you will need to consult a medical professional to determine safe weight loss goals and the development of a proper dietary plan. This ensures that as you go on with the Keto diet, your body does not suffer from the ill effects of prolonged Ketogenesis, especially if you happen to be Diabetic.

To start with the Keto diet however, your body will need to undergo a shift from the traditional consumption of carbohydrates and focus more on the consumption of proteins. Without carbohydrates, your body is now made to adjust its metabolism around the consumption of fats. Here, you can now expect Ketogenesis as your body, through the liver, begins to break down fat cells to obtain the glucose that is needed by your body. Your body, once it enters this state, has now entered a state called ketosis. Often, most dietitians find that ketosis is more easily attained when you fast, though again, if you choose to do so, only do this with professional medical advice. With the consumption of minimal carbohydrates and more protein, your body will continue to break down fat cells to ensure that it is able to obtain the glucose that it needs to fuel its needs.

1.2 Advantages of the Ketogenic Diet

There are several advantages to be had when you start off with the Keto diet. In this section, we touch upon the various advantages to be had when you opt to utilize this diet as your main means to lose weight.

1. Weight Reduction – it follows that when you lose weight with the Keto Diet, this also remedies the effects of obesity to a certain extent. From the descriptions of the various processes that have been provided for in the previous section, you would know now that the diet would ultimately break down the fat stores of your body as your body seeks to obtain the glucose that it needs for its metabolic processes. From this, as your body begins to break down the fat stores, the weight of the body is gradually reduced. One of the main concerns of this diet now is the maintenance of your appetite. However, because the diet of the body has shifted from the consumption of carbohydrates to the consumption of fats, the body begins to be easily satiated. This allows your body to more easily maintain the constant dietary pattern needed to help it lose weight.

2. Diabetes Mellitus Type II or Non-Insulin Dependent Diabetes Mellitus – it was mentioned earlier in this chapter that the use of the Keto Diet helps control the blood sugar levels or your glucose levels in your body. Studies on the effects of the Keto Diet have shown that persons who consume a low carb Ketogenic diet are less likely to be reliant on their medications. Additionally, laboratory tests conducted on those with the Keto Diet have shown that this diet is able to lower the amount of triglycerides (fats) in the bloodstream and lower the amount of Low-Density Lipoproteins (Bad Cholesterol) and raise the amount of High-Density Lipoproteins (Good Cholesterol).

3. Reduction of Malignancies – Cancer cells and tumors are fueled by large amounts of glucose. When you cut off a steady supply of readily available glucose through the reduction of carbohydrates in your diet, the cancer cells are essentially starved of the energy that they need to multiply and spread throughout the body. The cancer cells are unable to use the glucose that has been metabolized from the fat stores of the body, unlike the regular cells from the body.

4. Increased Mental Clarity- One of the advantages of the Keto Diet is that because of the amounts of glucose that it is able to generate, it is able to supply our brain with the adequate amounts of glucose needed. Additionally, the brain is able to run not only on glucose but on the ketones that are produced from the breakdown of fat stores in the body, and as a result, it has twice the amount of energy sources it needs to be able to function. This results in improved mental function.

5. Mood Stabilization – this results from the type of food you consume as part of the Ketogenic Diet. Because you need to control the types of food that you take in, and reduce the overall amount of refined and processed foods, your body is able to stabilize the neurotransmitters responsible for changes in mood, and as your blood sugar begins to stabilize, your mood is able to stabilize as well. This can be considered as an offshoot of the previous benefit where the brain has its function improved overall.

1.3 Consumption of Macronutrients

To understand how the Keto Diet differs from other diets when it comes to the consumption of macronutrients, it must be impressed that the Keto diet is reliant on a low-carbohydrate and a high fat, high protein diet. The goal of the diet is to ensure that the body is able to enter into a state of Ketosis that ranges from 0.5 to 5.0 mmols/L. To know if you are within this optimal level, you can easily use a home blood ketone screen test with the use of ketone test strips. To ensure that you do stay within this range however, here is a breakdown of how your diet should be broken down.

Carbohydrates – to get your Ketones to the minimum amount of 0.5 mmols/L requires restriction on the amount of carbohydrates used. This does not mean however that you should completely cut off carbohydrates from your diet. This is heavily dependent on your health status as each person has their own threshold at which their body is able to adequately maintain a state of ketosis without any harm caused upon the body. If you happen to be a healthy individual without any form of diabetes, your body will be able to tolerate 50 grams of carbohydrates in a single day. If you are diabetic however, or you have some form of impairment with how your body uses insulin, your carbohydrates are restricted to 20 to 30 grams in a day.

When you do choose carbohydrates to consume, it is essential that you are able to identify the carbohydrate components that increase your glucose and insulin levels. Fiber content is not an adequate measure of your carbohydrate consumption as it has no effect on your overall carbohydrate levels. To compute for this, you will need to look at the net carbohydrates – carbohydrate count from which the fiber and sugar alcohol are subtracted from. If the sugar alcohol is maltitol however, this should be included in the carbohydrate count.

Food options for carbohydrates do not include pasta, grains, potatoes, beans, desserts, sodas, juices and beer. Dairy options are limited, where you cannot choose dairy items that have high amounts of lactose- itself a form of sugar (a disaccharide of glucose and galactose to be precise). You are permitted to choose dairy items that are low in carbohydrates, such as hard cheeses, high-fat cheese, full-fat cheese, whipping cream and sour cream.

For a person who has no issues with diabetes or insulin impairments, a breakdown of 50 grams in a single day can be broken down into the sample seen below:

- 5 to 10 grams from proteins such as eggs, shellfish and cheese to include the addition of marinades and other flavors.
- 5 to 10 grams from vegetables
- 5 to 10 grams from nuts and seeds, as most tree nuts carry 5-6 grams per ounce.
- 5 to 10 grams from fruits and berries.
- 5 to 10 grams from low-carbohydrate sugar, high-fat dressings, or drinks with low sugar.

While you can follow this breakdown in variations provided you stay within the recommended range of 50 grams a day as per your nutritionist's recommendation, it is essential that you keep hydrated throughout your diet. Water, espresso and tea are excellent sources of hydration that keep you on the low-carb aspect of the Keto Diet. You may also use unsweetened almond milk and coconut milk. Diet beverages are not recommended as these contain various types of sugars. You are permitted a glass or two of wine, however, it is recommended that the wine be drier as this has a low sugar content.

Proteins- The focus of the Keto diet is on the effective use of proteins, enough to ensure that you do not lose muscle mass and tissue, while at the same time, prevent the inhibition of ketosis. You may ask why this may be the case for proteins? The consumption of excess proteins may lead to the inhibition of the ketosis state that your body needs to attain to make the Keto diet successful.

Adults however, require 0.5 to 1.5 grams of protein per kilogram per day to ensure that the body is able to maintain its ideal weight. The Keto diet produces weight loss through the reduction of the fat stores of the body, it does not cause an increase in the amount of protein already in the body. Computation of your protein consumption is then dependent on your ideal weight, and you will need the help of your nutritionist for this to ensure that you are able to obtain the correct measurements for a more precise computation.

For dieters who have no insulin issues, who use this diet for its neurological restoration properties and those who are generally athletic, the amount of protein should be as close to the lower limit permitted from the calculations. Otherwise, you may consume proteins in controlled moderation. Ideal protein sources include:

- Eggs at 6 to 8 grams per egg
- Grass-fed Meat, at 6 to 9 grams of protein per ounce of meat
- Omega-3 Rich Proteins such as Salmon and Anchovies, 6 to 9 grams of protein per ounce
- Tree Nuts and Seeds, which yield 4 to 8 grams of protein per ¼ cup (32 g)
- Vegetables, which yield 1 to 2 grams of protein per ounce

Fat- is the mainstay of the Keto diet and forms the bulk of the food consumed as part of the diet. If you consume enough fat, your body is able to maintain the bodyweight it needs without the need to breakdown proteins. Conversely, if you do require weight loss to take place, less fat should be consumed that the body may consume the fat stores that are present within it.

	To Maintain Weight	To Lose Weight
Carbohydrates	5-10%	5-10%
Protein	10-15%	10-15%
Dietary Fat	70-80%	35-40%
Stored Body Fat	0%	35-40%

The table above details how much of each macronutrient should comprise your food consumption. The percentages are dependent on your overall goals from your diet. It follows that for individuals who wish to maintain their current weight, they need to consume dietary fat to ensure that the body has an adequate supply of fat to break down. This is dependent upon the person as larger individuals may require more body fat. The amount of fat that you can consume in a single day is largely dependent on your gall bladder function however, as it is the organ that helps dispense the bile needed to emulsify the fats upon digestion. Bile salts would help augment the functions of the gall bladder.

When you do consume fat, it is best that you avoid the use of trans fats, and utilize fat sources from unsaturated fats such as Avocado Oil, Coconut Oil, Ghee, Full Cream, Olive Oil, Lard, and Medium-Chain Triglycerides, a form of fat source that can be easily broken down by the body to obtain glucose. Coconut oil is a good source of this.

1.4 Cautionary Measures

It is recommended that before you embark on the Keto diet that you seek a professional medical consultation with your physician and a nutritionist to help you determine the best way to start off your diet if your body is able to withstand the effects of ketosis. As a general rule, those who should exercise extra caution with the Keto Diet include the likes of:

- Persons who take Diabetes Medications as glucose levels may fluctuate in accordance with the reduction of carbohydrates from the diet.
- Persons who are on Hypertension Medications, as the pulse may fluctuate with a decrease in the amount of carbohydrates.
- Breastfeeding Mothers should not undertake this diet on a low-carb basis, as fat loss can be attained through the expression of breast milk as the baby feeds. It is recommended that

breastfeeding mothers should consume 50 grams of protein per day to maintain adequate nutritional levels.

- Kidney Disease patients should request for clearance from their physician before they embark on the diet.

2 CHAPTER II: THE KETO DIET SHOPPING LIST

As with most diets, there are unique restrictions on the types of food that are safe for you to consume to ensure that you are able to meet the nutritional needs of your body. This list is designed to help you stock up on supplies that ensure that your pantry is set to help you on your journey for the Ketogenic Diet. The portions for each item on the food list are dependent on the macronutrient proportions needed for your specific measurements. You can expect that there will be some computations needed on how much of each type of food you are allowed to consume so you can cross-check this list with your nutritionist to help you determine how much of each should last you for a week or so.

Proteins

- Albacore Tuna
- Anchovies
- Beef
- Chicken
- Clams
- Duck
- Eggs
- Goat
- Herring
- Lamb
- Mussels
- Natto
- Octopus
- Pork (to include Bacon, Prosciutto, Pancetta, Offal)
- Protein Powders (Egg, Egg White, Whey)- for Vegetarians
- Quail
- Salmon
- Sardines
- Scallops
- Shrimp
- Squid
- Tempeh
- Turkey
- Venison

Vegetables and Fruits (preferably those with no starch and are low-carb)

- Artichokes
- Asian Greens (Bok Choy, Pak Choy, Napa Cabbage)
- Asparagus
- Avocado
- Bean Sprouts
- Berries (Acai, Blackberries, Blueberries, Raspberries, Strawberries as examples)
- Capsicums
- Broccoli
- Broccolini
- Brussels Sprouts
- Cabbage (Sauerkraut and Kimchi included)
- Cauliflower
- Celery
- Collard Greens
- Cucumber
- Eggplant
- Garlic
- Green Beans
- Jicama
- Kale
- Kohlrabi
- Leeks
- Lettuce
- Mushrooms
- Radish
- Rutabaga
- Spaghetti Squash
- Spinach
- Tomatoes
- Zucchini

Dairy

- Hard Cheeses (Parmesan, Pecorino, Cheddar as examples)
- Butter
- Cottage Cheese
- Greek Yogurt (Plain)
- Heavy Cream
- Kefir
- Quark
- Skyr
- Sour Cream

Miscellaneous Items

- Avocado Oil
- Bacon Fat
- Chimichurri
- Cocoa Powder
- Coconut Aminos
- Coconut Oil
- Cream or Vinaigrette Based Dressings
- Dark Chocolate
- Dry Wine and Spirits (in limited amounts)
- Duck Fat
- Guacamole
- Hemp Oil
- Hot Sauce
- Hot Sauces
- Konjac Noodles
- Lard
- Lime Juice
- Low-Sugar Ketchup
- Mayonnaise
- Mustard
- Nuts (Almonds, Brazil Nuts, Cashews, Macadamia, Pecans, Pistachios, Walnuts)
- Olive Oil
- Pesto
- Sambal Oelek
- Seeds (Chia Seeds, Flax Seeds, Hemp Seeds, Poppy Seeds, Pumpkin Seeds, Sesame Seeds and Tahini)
- Sesame Oil
- Shirataki Noodles (as a pasta and noodle substitute)
- Tallow
- Unsweetened Coffee and Tea
- Unsweetened Plant Milk (Almond and Coconut)
- Vinegar
- Worcestershire Sauce

Baking Supplies

- Almond Meal
- Cocoa Butter
- Coconut Flour
- Collagen
- Erythritol
- Flax Meal
- Gelatin
- Most spices and herbs
- Peanut Flour
- Pink Salt
- Psyllium Husk
- Stevia
- Vanilla
- Xanthan Gum
- Xylitol

There are some items that may be used in moderation, but this is dependent on the carbohydrate count, especially for most fruits and vegetables. You will want to avoid certain food items such as honey, sugar and maple syrup due to their high carbohydrate count, as well as complex starches such as pasta, potatoes, sweet potatoes and beets. While there are other food items that may be added to the list, it is important that their overall net carbohydrate count to determine if they are safe. Refer to Chapter I on the Consumption of Macronutrients to determine what a reasonable amount of carbohydrates to consume is. The list above is not completely exhaustive, and some items may not be available at your local grocers, or are quite pricey. Work within your budget and you will still be able to produce high quality Keto-friendly meals.

3 BREAKFAST RECIPES

3.1 Bacon, Cheese and Chive Scones

Serves: 15 Prep Time: 15 minutes Cook Time: 25 minutes

Ingredients:

- Flax Seeds, ¼ cup (32 g)
- Almond Meal, 1 ½ cups (350 ml)
- Baking Powder, 1 teaspoon (5ml)
- Coconut Flour, ¼ cup (32 g)
- Chives, 3 tablespoons (45 ml), finely chopped
- Cheddar Cheese, 1.8 oz., shredded
- Black Pepper, freshly ground, ½ teaspoon (2.5 ml)
- Salt, ¼ teaspoon (1.25 ml)
- Bacon, 4 slices
- Unsweetened Almond Milk, 3 tablespoons (45 ml),
- Eggs, 2 medium pieces

Procedure:

1. Heat up an oven to 375 degrees Fahrenheit. Line a baking sheet with parchment paper and set aside.
2. In a blender, grind the flaxseeds. Mix the ground flaxseed, Almond Meal, coconut flour, baking powder, cheese, chives, salt and pepper into a bowl. Chop the bacon and cook for 3-4 minutes until browned. Let cool.
3. Add the eggs into a cup and whisk in the almond milk until well blended. Mix this into the flour mixture slowly. Add the chopped bacon and mix thoroughly until bacon is incorporated.
4. Roll the scone dough in between sheets of greaseproof paper until it reaches an even thickness. Cut 15 pieces of scones from the dough. Arrange on the baking tray and bake for 15 minutes. Sprinkle cheese on top and bake for 10 more minutes or until the cheese has liquefied. Serve immediately or store.

Nutritional Facts: Cal: 127; Carb: 1.3g; Protein: 5.7g; Fat: 2.3g; Fiber: 2.2g; Sugars: 6.8g; Cholesterol: 366mg; Sodium: 2709mg

3.2 Tomatillo Keto Muffins

Serves: 10 Prep Time: 15 minutes Cook Time: 30 minutes

Ingredients:

- Bacon Drippings, 2 tablespoons (30 ml)
- Beef Jerky Manchaca, 1 oz.,
- Almond Meal, ½ cup (118 ml)
- Tomatillo Salsa, ½ cup (118 ml)
- Eggs, 4 medium pieces

Procedure:

1. Heat up an oven to 350 degrees Fahrenheit. Line a muffin tin with paper liners and set aside.
2. In a non-stick skillet, liquefy the bacon drippings and cook the Manchaca. Stir until it has softened and fully cooked. Let cool for about five minutes.
3. Add the cooked Manchaca into a food processor and add the Almond Meal, eggs and tomatillo salsa. Blend for 30 seconds until well incorporated and pour into the prepared muffin tray.
4. Bake for 30 minutes or until a skewer inserted into the center of the muffin comes out clean. Serve immediately or store.

Nutritional Facts: Cal: 128; Carb: 2.5g; Protein: 6.6g; Fat: 10g; Fiber: 0.75g; Sugars: 3.9g; Cholesterol: 710mg; Sodium: 1971mg

3.3 Pesto Egg Muffins

Serves: 10 Prep Time: 15 minutes Cook Time: 30 minutes

Ingredients:

- Frozen Spinach, 2/3 cup, thawed and drained
- Olives, ½ cup (118 ml), pitted
- Sun Dried Tomatoes, ¼ cup (32 g), chopped
- Eggs, 6 medium pieces
- Pesto, 3 tablespoons (45 ml)
- Salt
- Black Pepper, freshly ground
- Goat Cheese, 4.4 oz.

Procedure:

1. Heat up an oven to 350 degrees Fahrenheit. Prepare a muffin tray with muffin liners or grease with a non-stick Cook spray. Set aside.
2. Squeeze excess water from the spinach and slice the olives. Chop the sun dried tomatoes and set aside. Crack the eggs into a bowl, and season with the salt and pepper. Add the pesto and whisk until well incorporated.
3. Crumble the goat cheese into the prepared muffin tins and layer the prepared spinach, olives and sun dried tomatoes. Pour the egg mixture on top and bake for 25 minutes or until egg has set.
4. Serve immediately or store for five days.

Nutritional Facts: Cal: 125; Carb: 1.2g; Protein: 6.9g; Fat: 10.2g; Fiber: 0.7g; Sugars: 6.1g; Cholesterol: 1117mg; Sodium: 1487mg

3.4 Quick and Easy Keto Breakfast

Serves: 2 Prep Time: 15 minutes Cook Time: 15 minutes

Ingredients:

- Bacon, 4 strips
- Eggs, 2 large
- Sea Salt, ¼ teaspoon (1.25 ml)
- Avocado, 1 large, pitted, peeled and sliced thinly

Procedure:

1. Add the bacon and avocado into a skillet and cook over a medium setting for 3 minutes until the bacon is fully browned and the fat has rendered. Remove from the pan but leave the rendered bacon fat in the pan.
2. Fry the eggs to their desired doneness in the bacon fat and season with salt. Serve immediately.

Nutritional Facts: Cal: 313; Carb: 2.5g; Protein: 13g; Fat: 26g; Fiber: 6g; Sugars: 0.9g; Cholesterol: 228mg; Sodium: 1012mg

3.5 Green Eggs

Serves: 1 Prep Time: 10 minutes Cook Time: 10 minutes

Ingredients:

- Eggs, 3 large
- Pesto, 1 tablespoon (15 ml)
- Butter, 1 tablespoon (15 ml)
- Coconut Cream, 2 tablespoons (30 ml)
- Salt
- Black Pepper, freshly ground

Procedure:

1. Crack the eggs into a bowl and whisk together. Season with salt and black pepper. Pour the eggs into a pan. Add the butter and switch the flame on a medium setting. Stir well and add the pesto. Remove the eggs from the heat and stir in the creamed coconut milk. Set back on the heat and cook until the eggs are done. Serve immediately.

Nutritional Facts: Cal: 467; Carb: 2.6g; Protein: 20.4g; Fat: 41.5g; Fiber: 0.7g; Sugars: 1.7g; Cholesterol: 591mg; Sodium: 498mg

3.6 Nutty Baked Brie

Serves: 1 Prep Time: 15 minutes Cook Time: 20 minutes

Ingredients:

- Prosciutto, 1 slice, ½ oz.,
- Brie Cheese, full fat, 1 oz.,
- Pecan Halves, 6 pieces
- Black Pepper, 1/8 teaspoon (0.6g)

Procedure:

1. Heat up an oven to 350 degrees and prepare a muffin tin with non-stick Cook spray. Layer the prosciutto on the bottom of the muffin tin. Slice in half if needed.
2. Cube the brie. Leave the rind on. Arrange in the prepared muffin tin. Arrange the halved pecans on the brie. Bake for 12 minutes or until the brie has liquefied. Let cool before eating.

Nutritional Facts: Cal: 183; Carb: 0.43g; Protein: 8.42g; Fat: 16.5g; Fiber: 1g; Sugars: 1.6g; Cholesterol: 51mg; Sodium: 689mg

3.7 Buttered Herb Eggs

Serves: 2 Prep Time: 10 minutes Cook Time: 20 minutes

Ingredients:

- Butter,2 tablespoons (30 ml)
- Coconut Oil, 1 tablespoon (15 ml)
- Garlic, 2 cloves, peeled and minced
- Thyme Leaves, fresh, 1 teaspoon (5ml)
- Cilantro, ½ cup (43 g), chopped
- Parsley Leaves, ½ cup (32 g), fresh, chopped
- Eggs, 4 medium
- Cayenne Pepper, ¼ teaspoon (1.25 ml)
- Dried Cumin Seed, ¼ teaspoon (1.25 ml)ground
- Sea Salt

Procedure:

1. Liquefy the butter and coconut oil in a skillet over a medium setting. Sauté the garlic for 3 minutes until it begins to brown. Add the thyme and cook for 30 seconds. Stir to make sure it does not burn. Add the parsley and cilantro and cook for 3 minutes until wilted but not burned.

2. Add the eggs, keep the yolks intact. Season with the cayenne, cumin and salt. Cover with a lid and lower the heat to low. Cook for 4-6 minutes until yolks have just set. Serve immediately.

Nutritional Facts: Cal: 311; Carb: 2.5g; Protein: 12.8g; Fat: 27.5g; Fiber: 1g; Sugars: 1g; Cholesterol: 358mg; Sodium: 450mg

3.8 Garden Hash

Serves: 1 Prep Time: 10 minutes Cook Time: 20 minutes

Ingredients:

- Onion, ½ piece, small, chopped
- Bacon, 2 slices
- Coconut Oil, 1 tablespoon (15 ml)
- Zucchini, 1 medium piece, chopped
- Chives, 1 tablespoon (15 ml), finely chopped
- Egg, 1 large
- Salt, ¼ teaspoon (1.25 ml)

Procedure:

1. Heat the coconut oil in a skillet over a medium setting and sauté the onions for 3 minutes until softened. Cook the bacon in the same pan until it has lightly browned. Add the chopped zucchini into the pan and cook for 10-15 minutes until it has softened. Remove from heat and season with the chives.

2. In a separate egg, fry the egg and season with salt. Top the vegetable mix with the fried egg and serve immediately.

Nutritional Facts: Cal: 423; Carb: 6.6g; Protein: 17.4g; Fat: 35.5g; Fiber: 2.5g; Sugars: 5.3g; Cholesterol: 205mg; Sodium: 1116mg

3.9 Sea Skipper's Eggs

Serves: 1 Prep Time: 10 minutes Cook Time: 10 minutes

Ingredients:

- Sardines in Olive Oil. 5 to 6 grams
- Eggs, 2 medium
- Marinated Artichoke Hearts, 2 ½ tablespoons (37.5 g)
- Arugula Leaves, ½ cup (43 g)
- Salt
- Pepper

Procedure:

1. Heat up an oven to 375 degrees Fahrenheit. Layer the sardines at the bottom of an ovenproof dish. Carefully crack the eggs on top to cover the sardines and top with the artichoke hearts and arugula. Season with salt and pepper. Bake for 10 minutes and serve immediately.

Nutritional Facts: Cal: 315; Carb: 3.5g; Protein: 28g; Fat: 20.63g; Fiber: 1.3g; Sugars: 1.1g; Cholesterol: 327mg; Sodium: 408mg

3.10 Buffalo Chicken Breakfast Cups

Serves: 12 pieces (2 per serving) Prep Time: 5 minutes Cook Time: 20 minutes

Ingredients:

- Cooked Chicken, 1 cup (237 ml), shredded (185 grams)
- Eggs, 8 large
- Ghee, ¼ cup (32 g) (32 g) plus 2 tablespoons (30 ml)
- Scallions, 4 pieces, finely chopped
- Hot Sauce, 1 tablespoon (15 ml)
- Garlic Powder, 2 teaspoons (10 ml)
- Salt
- Pepper

Procedure:

1. Heat up the oven to 375 degrees Fahrenheit and line a 12-cup muffin pan with paper liners. You may use a silicone muffin tray if available, but do not line anymore.

2. Add all of the ingredients into a bowl and stir until well incorporated. Pour the batter into the prepared muffin trays until ¾ of the way full. Bake for 20 minutes or until a skewer inserted into the center of the cups comes out clean. Serve immediately or store for up to 5 days.

Nutritional Facts: Cal: 269; Carb: 1.5g; Protein: 17.8g; Fat: 21.2g; Fiber: 0.4g; Sugars: 1g; Cholesterol: 272mg; Sodium: 155mg

3.11 Italian Ham Biscuits

Serves: 12 (2 per serving) Prep Time: 10 minutes Cook Time: 20 minutes

Ingredients:

- Mayonnaise, ¾ cup (175 ml)
- Eggs, 6 large pieces
- Coconut Flour, 1 cup (237 ml)
- Baking Powder, 1 ½ teaspoons (5.9 g)
- Prosciutto, 12 pieces or 3.5 oz., finely chopped
- Scallions, 3 pieces, finely chopped

Procedure:

1. Heat up an oven to 375 degrees Fahrenheit and prepare a baking sheet with baking parchment or a silicone pad.
2. Whisk the eggs and mayonnaise in a mixing bowl to combine. In a separate bowl, mix the baking powder and coconut flour until evenly mixed. Pour the mayonnaise mixture into the flour mix and stir until well incorporated. Carefully fold the prosciutto and scallions into the mix until well incorporated.
3. Shape the dough into 12 even pieces and roll a piece between your palms. Place on the prepared baking sheet and press until an inch thick, Repeat with the other pieces and bake for 15 to 20 minutes until golden brown. Remove from oven and let cool slightly before serving or storing. May be stored for 3 days in the fridge or for a month in the freezer.

Nutritional Facts: Cal: 299; Carb: 2.9g; Protein: 10.9g; Fat: 27.4g; Fiber: 1.1g; Sugars: 0.7g; Cholesterol: 208mg; Sodium: 567mg

3.12 Basic Biscuit in a Mug Recipe

Serves: 1 Prep Time: 1 minute Cook Time: 2 minutes

Ingredients:

- Cider Vinegar, 1 teaspoon (5ml)
- Coconut Oil, 1 tablespoon (15 ml)
- Egg, 1 large
- Salt
- Baking Powder, ½ teaspoon (2.5 ml)
- Coconut Flour, 1 tablespoon (15 ml)
- Blanched Almond Meal, ¼ cup (32 g)

Procedure:

1. Add all of the ingredients into a microwave-safe mug with a 2 inch wide base. Mix until fully incorporated and press down the dough with a spoon.
2. Place the mug in a microwave and cook on high for 1 minute and 30 seconds. Remove from the microwave and insert a toothpick. If it comes out clean, allow to cool. If sticky, cook for 15-30 seconds.
3. Turn the mug over on a plate and shake the biscuit loose. Spread with butter or coconut oil while warm if desired. You may store in the fridge for 3 days or in the freezer for 2 months.

Nutritional Facts: Cal: 399; Carb: 10.6g; Protein: 13.8g; Fat: 33.5g; Fiber: 5.5g; Sugars: 1.9g; Cholesterol: 164mg; Sodium: 535mg

3.13 Chocolate Coconut Granola

Serves: 3 ½ cups Prep Time: 5 minutes Cook Time: 10 minutes plus 20 minutes to cool

Ingredients:

- Cinnamon, 1 teaspoon (5ml), ground
- Erythritol, 1/3 cup (75 ml)
- Water, 2 tablespoons (30 ml)
- Vanilla, 1 teaspoon (5ml)
- Cocoa Powder, 1/3 cup (75 ml)
- Salt
- Unsweetened Coconut Flakes, 3 cups (360 g)

Procedure:

1. Line a baking sheet with baking parchment or a silicone pad and set aside.
2. Add the erythritol, water and vanilla into a saucepan and heat over a medium low flame. Allow to simmer and stir every 30 seconds. Lower the heat to low and add the cocoa powder, cinnamon and salt. Stir until well incorporated. Add the coconut flakes and stir until well incorporated. Cook for 6-7 minutes until the bottom of the pan becomes sticky.
3. Remove from heat and pour onto the prepared baking sheet. Let cool for 20 minutes before cutting. Serve immediately or store for 10 days in the fridge or a month in the freezer.

Nutritional Facts: Cal: 106; Carb: 5g; Protein: 0.9g; Fat: 9.2g; Fiber: 2.7g; Sugars: 0.9g; Cholesterol: 0mg; Sodium: 106mg

3.14 Pumpkin Spiced Overnight Breakfast

Serves: 2 minutes Prep Time: 5 minutes Waiting Time: 8 hours to soak

Ingredients:

- Hemp Seeds, ½ cup, hulled
- Milk, 1/3 cup (75 ml), non-dairy or regular
- Coffee, ½ cup, brewed decaffeinated
- Pumpkin Puree, 2 tablespoons (30 ml)
- Cloves, 1/8 teaspoon (0.6g), ground
- Chia Seeds, 1 tablespoon (15 ml)s
- Cinnamon, ½ teaspoon (2.5 ml), ground
- Erythritol, 2 teaspoons (10 ml)
- Vanilla, ½ teaspoon (2.5 ml)
- Nutmeg, ¼ teaspoon (1.25 ml) ground
- Salt
- Roasted Pecans, chopped, for topping
- Toasted Unsweetened Shredded Coconut, for topping
- Hemp Seeds to top
- Cinnamon to top

Procedure:

1. Add all of the ingredients into a 12 oz. or larger container and stir until well combined. Cover and store in the refrigerator to soak overnight or for 8 hours.
2. To serve: Add more milk until the oats reaches your desired consistency. Portion into two bowls and top with your desired toppings. Serve.

Nutritional Facts: Cal: 337; Carb: 9.4g; Protein: 15g; Fat: 26.7g; Fiber: 6.8g; Sugars: 1.4g; Cholesterol: 0mg; Sodium: 89mg

4 SALADS

4.1 Spinach with Cauliflower Tabbouleh

Serves: 6 Prep Time: 10 minutes Cook Time: 20 minutes

Ingredients:

- Coconut Oil, 2 tablespoons (30 ml)
- Cauliflower Rice, 3 cups (360 g)
- Spinach, 3 cups (360 g), chopped
- Mint, ½ cup, freshly chopped
- Parsley Leaves, fresh, 1 cup (237 ml), chopped
- Scallions, 2 pieces, finely chopped
- Cucumber, 1 medium piece, seeded and chopped
- Cherry Tomatoes, 1 cup (237 ml), chopped
- Salt
- Black Pepper, freshly ground
- Garlic, 1 clove, peeled and minced
- Olive Oil, ½ cup
- Lemon Juice, ½ cup, freshly squeezed

Procedure:

1. Heat the coconut oil in a skillet over a medium setting. Add the cauliflower rice and season with salt. Allow to cook for five minutes and set aside in a bowl to cool.
2. In a bowl, add the tomatoes, cucumber, scallions, parsley, and mint. Add the chopped spinach into the bowl with the cauliflower rice and toss to mix evenly.
3. To make the dressing, in a separate bowl, mix the lemon juice, olive oil and garlic and whisk until fully combined. Season with black pepper.
4. Combine the vegetables with the cauliflower rice mixture and toss until well combined. Pour the dressing over the mix and toss once more to coat the vegetables with the dressing. Serve immediately.

Nutritional Facts: Cal: 245; Carb: 5.4g; Protein: 2.6g; Fat: 23.5g; Fiber: 3g; Sugars: 2.8g; Cholesterol: 0mg; Sodium: 90mg

4.2 Greek Salad

Serves: 4 Prep Time: 10 minutes Cook Time: 0 minutes

Ingredients:

- Tomatoes, 4 medium pieces, sliced
- Onion, 1 small, sliced
- Capsicum, 1 small, seeded and sliced
- Cucumber, 1 large, peeled, seeded and chopped
- Feta Cheese, 7 oz.,
- Oregano Leaves, dried, 1 teaspoon (5ml)
- Olives, 16 pieces, pitted
- Capers, 4 tablespoons
- Olive Oil, 4 tablespoons
- Salt
- Black Pepper, freshly ground

Procedure:

1. Add the chopped and prepared vegetables into a bowl. Add the oregano leaves, olives and capers. Crumble the feta all over the salad. Drizzle the salad with olive oil and season with salt and pepper. Toss to combine and serve.

Nutritional Facts: Cal: 323; Carb: 8g; Protein: 9.3g; Fat: 27.8g; Fiber: 3.3g; Sugars: 6.1g; Cholesterol: 44mg; Sodium: 963mg

4.3 Brussels Sprouts Salad

Serves: 1 Prep Time: 5 minutes Cook Time: 0 minutes

Ingredients:

- Brussels Sprouts, 1 cup (237 ml), chopped
- Olive Oil. 2 tablespoons (30 ml)
- Lemon Juice, 1 tablespoon (15 ml), freshly squeezed
- Black Pepper, freshly ground

Procedure:

1. Add all of the ingredients into a bowl and toss before you serve to coat the Brussels sprouts in the vinaigrette.

Nutritional Facts: Cal: 323; Carb: 8g; Protein: 9.3g; Fat: 27.8g; Fiber: 3.3g; Sugars: 6.1g; Cholesterol: 44mg; Sodium: 963mg

4.4 Mediterranean Appetizer Salad

Serves: 4 Prep Time: 10 minutes Cook Time: 0 minutes

Ingredients:

- Roasted Red Peppers, 1 (12 oz.,) jar, drained and chopped roughly
- Marinated Artichoke Hearts, 1 (6.5 oz.) jar, drained and quartered
- Cremini or Chestnut Mushrooms, 1 (4 oz.,) can, drained and sliced
- Salami, 4 oz. (0.11 kg)diced
- Capers, 3 tablespoons (45 ml), drained from brine
- Vinaigrette, ¾ cup (175 ml)

Procedure:

1. Add all of the ingredients into a bowl and toss to coat with the dressing. Serve immediately.

Nutritional Facts: Cal: 433; Carb: 13.5g; Protein: 7.3g; Fat: 38.9g; Fiber: 4.4g; Sugars: 5g; Cholesterol: 20mg; Sodium: 1335mg

4.5 Quick Pantry Salad

Serves: 1 Prep Time: 10 minutes Cook Time: 0 minutes

Ingredients:

- Romaine Lettuce, 1 small head, chopped
- Cherry Tomatoes, 8 pieces, halved
- Cucumber, half a piece, peeled, seeded and chopped
- Celery, 1 stalk, chopped
- Black Olives, ¼ cup (32 g) , pitted and chopped
- Onions, 2 tablespoons (30 ml), peeled and diced
- Mint Leaves, 2 tablespoons (30 ml), chopped
- Vinaigrette, ¼ cup (32 g)

Procedure:

1. Layer the lettuce into a bowl and top with the remainder of the vegetables. Toss with the vinaigrette until evenly coated. Serve immediately.

Nutritional Facts: Cal: 476; Carb: 18g; Protein: 6.5g; Fat: 42g; Fiber: 6.5g; Sugars: 7.1g; Cholesterol: 0mg; Sodium: 608mg

4.6 Salad Greens with Ginger Vinaigrette

Serves: 1 Prep Time: 10 minutes Cook Time: 0 minutes

Ingredients:

- Lemon Juice, ¼ cup (32 g) freshly squeezed
- Olive Oil, 2 tablespoons (30 ml) plus 2 teaspoons (10 ml)
- Ginger, 1 teaspoon (5ml)s, freshly peeled and minced, or grated
- Garlic, 2 cloves, peeled and minced
- Salt
- Black Pepper, freshly ground
- Kale Leaves, 1 cup (237 ml), midrib removed, leaves roughly chopped, wash with hot water
- Mesclun Salad Greens, 3 cups (360 g)
- Hemp Seeds, ¼ cup (32 g) hulled
- Cilantro Leaves, 1 bunch, finely chopped
- Parsley Leaves, 1 bunch, chopped
- Mint Leaves, 1 handful, chopped

Procedure:

1. Add all of the vegetables into a bowl and set aside. In a separate bowl, whisk together the lemon juice, olive oil, ginger, garlic, salt and pepper to make the vinaigrette. Add the vinaigrette into the vegetables and toss. Serve immediately.

Nutritional Facts: Cal: 496; Carb: 23g; Protein: 9.3g; Fat: 40.8g; Fiber: 5.6g; Sugars: 4.4g; Cholesterol: 0mg; Sodium: 187mg

4.7 Kale Salad with Tropical Sesame Dressing

Serves: 4 Prep Time: 15 minutes Cook Time: 0 minutes

Ingredients:

- Avocado Oil, ½ cup
- Lime Juice, ¼ cup (32 g)
- Tahini, ¼ cup (32 g)
- Garlic, 2 cloves, minced
- Jalapeno Pepper, 1 piece, seeded and diced
- Cilantro Leaves, 5 sprigs, chopped
- Dried Cumin Seed, ½ teaspoon (2.5 ml), ground
- Salt
- Red Pepper Flakes, ¼ teaspoon (1.25 ml)
- Kale Leaves, 6 cups (1419.5 g), midrib removed, leaves chopped and rinsed in hot water to soften
- Radishes, 1 dozen, thinly sliced
- Capsicum, 1 piece, seeded and chopped
- Avocado, 1 medium fruit, peeled, pitted and cubed
- Pumpkin Seeds, ¼ cup (32 g)

Procedure:

1. In a bowl, whisk together the avocado oil, lime juice, tahini, garlic, jalapeno, cilantro, cumin, salt and red pepper flakes to form the dressing. Set aside.
2. Dry the rinsed kale leaves and add with the remainder of the vegetables and pumpkin seeds into a bowl. Toss with the dressing to coat the vegetables and serve immediately. You may store for 5 days in the fridge but do not add the avocado until the last minute.

Nutritional Facts: Cal: 517; Carb: 11.5g; Protein: 10.7g; Fat: 47g; Fiber: 9.4g; Sugars: 3.9g; Cholesterol: 0mg; Sodium: 373mg

4.8 Zucchini Spiral Salad

Serves: 4 Prep Time: 5 minutes Cook Time: 0 minutes

Ingredients:

- Zucchinis, 4 medium pieces, spiralized
- Black Olives, 12 oz., pitted and halved lengthwise
- Cherry Tomatoes, 1 pint, halved lengthwise
- Pine Nuts, ½ cup
- Sesame Seeds, ¼ cup (32 g) plus 2 tablespoons (30 ml)
- Creamy Italian Dressing, 2/3 cup

Procedure:

1. Add all of the ingredients into a mixing bowl and toss to coat in the dressing. Portion evenly into bowls and serve immediately.

Nutritional Facts: Cal: 562; Carb: 13.5g; Protein: 8.9g; Fat: 53g; Fiber: 8.5g; Sugars: 6.7g; Cholesterol: 2.7mg; Sodium: 886mg

4.9 German Rutabaga Salad

Serves: 5 Prep Time: 10 minutes Cook Time: 10 minutes

Ingredients:

- Rutabagas, 2 medium sized pieces, peeled
- Salt
- Red Onion, 1 small piece, finely diced
- Cider Vinegar, ¼ cup (32 g)
- Olive Oil, ¼ cup (32 g)
- Scallions, 4 stalks, sliced thinly
- Dijon Mustard, 1 tablespoon (15 ml)
- Erythritol, 1 teaspoon (5ml)
- Black Pepper

Procedure:

1. Cube the rutabaga into 1-inch pieces and add them into a large saucepan with enough water to cover them. Season with salt and cover with a lid. Allow the water to boil on high. Reduce the flame to a simmer and allow to cook for 10 minutes until it can be pierced with a fork.
2. While the rutabagas cook, add the remainder of the ingredients into a salad bowl and toss to combine. Drain the rutabagas and add them to the salad bowl. Toss once more to coat the rutabaga in the vinaigrette.
3. Mix 1 ½ tablespoons each of Dijon Mustard and Mayonnaise in a small bowl. Use this to garnish the salad with slices of ham or other deli meats.

Nutritional Facts: Cal: 296; Carb: 14g; Protein: 14g; Fat: 18.8g; Fiber: 5g; Sugars: 10g; Cholesterol: 33mg; Sodium: 1377mg

4.10 Salmon Salad Rolls

Serves: 4 Prep Time: 10 minutes Cook Time: 0 minutes

Ingredients:

- Canned Salmon, 1 (12 oz.) can, with no salt
- Horseradish Dressing, 3 tablespoons (45 ml)
- Dill Leaves, fresh, 1 tablespoon (15 ml)
- Lemon Juice, 2 teaspoons (10 ml)
- Salt
- Black Pepper
- Butter Lettuce Leaves, 12 pieces, rinsed
- Mayonnaise, ½ cup

Procedure:

1. Add the salmon, horseradish, dill, lemon juice, salt and pepper into a bowl and stir until thoroughly mixed. Arrange the lettuce leaves on a platter and top each with two tablespoons of the salmon mixture. Top this with two teaspoons of mayonnaise per leaf and serve immediately.

Nutritional Facts: Cal: 314; Carb: 3.3g; Protein: 14.6g; Fat: 26.5g; Fiber: 1.1g; Sugars: 1.8g; Cholesterol: 33mg; Sodium: 526mg

4.11 Curried Chicken Salad

Serves: 6 Prep Time: 10 minutes Cook Time: 15 minutes

Ingredients:

- Chicken Breasts, 1 ½ pounds, deboned and skinned, cooked and diced
- Celery, 2 medium stalks, chopped
- Onion, ½ medium piece, peeled and minced
- Walnuts, ½ cup, lightly toasted
- Black Pepper
- Curry Powder, ½ teaspoon (2.5 ml)
- Coconut Oil Mayonnaise, ¾ cup (175 ml)

Procedure:

1. Add all of the ingredients into a bowl and stir until well combined. Portion each into six equal portions and store for up to a week.

Nutritional Facts: Cal: 206; Carb: 2g; Protein: 26g; Fat: 9g; Fiber: 1g; Sugars: 1g; Cholesterol: 19mg; Sodium: 68mg

4.12 Caesar Salad

Serves: 4 Prep Time: 15 minutes Cook Time: 0 minutes

Ingredients:

- Cider Vinegar, 3 tablespoons (45 ml)
- Egg Yolk, 1 piece
- Dijon Mustard, 1 teaspoon (5ml)
- Avocado Oil, 8 tablespoons
- Garlic, 2 cloves, peeled and minced
- Parmesan Cheese, 4 tablespoons, shredded
- Anchovies, 4 fillets
- Romaine Hearts, 24 pieces
- Pork Rinds, 2 oz., chopped

Procedure:

1. Add the cider vinegar, egg yolk and mustard in a blender. Pour the avocado oil and blend on low. Add the garlic, grated parmesan and anchovies and blend until smooth.
2. Drizzle on the leaves and garnish with the pork rinds and shaved or grated parmesan.

Nutritional Facts: Cal: 727; Carb: 1.8g; Protein: 13g; Fat: 38.75g; Fiber: 0.5g; Sugars: 0.8g; Cholesterol: 89mg; Sodium: 1031mg

5 SOUPS AND STEWS

5.1 Oriental Broccoli Soup

Serves: 4 Prep Time: 5 minutes Cook Time: 25 minutes

Ingredients:

- Coconut Oil, 3 tablespoons (45 ml)
- Onion, 1 small white, peeled and sliced
- Garlic, 2 cloves, peeled and minced
- Broccoli Florets, 5 cups (1182.9 g)
- Coconut Milk, 1 (13 oz.) can
- Chicken Stock, 1 ½ cups (350 ml)
- Ginger Root, 1 2-inch piece, peeled and grated
- Turmeric, ground, 1 ½ teaspoons (5.9 g)
- Salt
- Collagen Peptides (optional)
- Sesame Seeds, ¼ cup (32 g)

Procedure:

1. Heat the coconut oil in a saucepan over a medium setting and sauté the onion and garlic. Cook until they are translucent, about 10 minutes. Make sure the garlic does not burn. Add the broccoli florets, coconut milk, stock, ginger, turmeric and salt. Cover with a lid and cook for 15 minutes until the broccoli has softened.
2. Add this into a food processor or blender and blend until smooth. If you use the collagen peptides, you may add them to the soup at this point. Once smooth, portion these out into bowls and garnish with a tablespoon of sesame seeds. Serve immediately.

Nutritional Facts: Cal: 344; Carb: 7.9g; Protein: 13.3g; Fat: 26.8g; Fiber: 4.5g; Sugars: 2.9g; Cholesterol: 4mg; Sodium: 548mg

5.2 Sauerkraut and Trimmings in a Bowl

Serves: 4 Prep Time: 2 minutes Cook Time: 25 minutes

Ingredients:

- Beef Mince, 1 pound (0.45 kg)
- Onion, 1 small piece, peeled and sliced thinly
- Garlic, 1 clove, minced
- Dried Cumin Seed, ground, 1 ½ teaspoons (5.9 g)
- Beef Stock, 3 cups (360 g)
- Sauerkraut, 1 cup (237 ml)
- Salt

Procedure:

1. In a saucepan, add the beef mince, onion, garlic and cumin and heat over a medium setting. Sauté until the onion is translucent, for about 10 minutes. Pour in the broth and sauerkraut and season with the salt. Cover with a lid and cook for 15 minutes until the onion has softened and the soup is aromatic. Portion evenly into bowls and serve immediately.

Nutritional Facts: Cal: 469; Carb: 7.7g; Protein: 48.8g; Fat: 27g; Fiber: 2.2g; Sugars: 3.9g; Cholesterol: 131mg; Sodium: 4150mg

5.3 Coconut Chicken Curry Soup

Serves: 4 Prep Time: 10 minutes Cook Time: 20 minutes

Ingredients:

- Red Curry Paste, 1/3 cup (75 ml)
- Coconut Milk, 1 cup (237 ml)
- Chicken Stock, 2 cups (475 ml)
- Chicken Thighs, 1 pound (0.45 kg), boneless, skinless and cut into cubes
- Ginger, 1 2-inch piece, peeled and grated
- Garlic, 2 cloves, minced
- Coconut Oil, ¼ cup (32 g)
- Salt
- Zucchini, 2 medium pieces, spiralized
- Scallions, 3 stalks, sliced thinly
- Cilantro Leaves, ¼ cup (32 g), chopped

Procedure:

1. Heat the coconut oil in a medium saucepan over a medium setting. Sauté the garlic and ginger until aromatic for about 2 minutes. Make sure they aren't burned. Add the cubed chicken thighs, chicken stock, coconut milk, red curry paste, and salt. Stir to combine and cover. Bring the soup to a simmer over a medium high flame. Once it simmers, lower the heat to low and allow to simmer for 15 minutes.
2. Portion the spiralized Zucchinis into four bowls and pour the soup. Garnish with the scallions and cilantro. Serve immediately, or freeze for up to a month. It may keep in the fridge for 3 days.

Nutritional Facts: Cal: 567; Carb: 9.8g; Protein: 40g; Fat: 40.3g; Fiber: 1.5g; Sugars: 3g; Cholesterol: 101mg; Sodium: 168mg

5.4 Mexican Chicken Soup

Serves: 4 Prep Time: 5 minutes Cook Time: 20 minutes

Ingredients:

- Cilantro Leaves
- Avocadoes, 2 medium fruits, pitted, peeled and thinly sliced
- Avocado Oil, ¼ cup (32 g)
- Cheddar Cheese, 1 cup (237 ml), shredded (optional)
- Salt
- Spanish Paprika, 1 teaspoon (5ml)
- Onion, 1 small white, peeled and diced
- Oregano Leaves, dried, 1 teaspoon (5ml)
- Dried Cumin Seed, 1 teaspoon (5ml), ground
- Garlic, 2 cloves, peeled and minced
- Red Capsicum, 1 whole, seeded and diced
- Chicken Breasts, 1 pound (0.45 kg), boneless, skinless and sliced thinly
- Fire-Roasted Whole Tomatoes, 1 (14.5 oz.) can
- Chicken Stock, 1 ½ cups (350 ml)
- Coconut Milk, 1 cup (237 ml)
- Cider Vinegar, 1 tablespoon (15 ml)

Procedure:

1. Heat the avocado oil in a large saucepan over a medium setting. Sauté the onions, garlic, and Capsicums until they have softened and are aromatic, for about 5 minutes. Add the chicken, tomatoes, stock, coconut milk, vinegar, cumin, oregano, Spanish paprika and salt. Stir to combine and cover. Bring to a simmer over a medium high flame. Once it has reached a simmer, lower the heat to low and allow to simmer for 15 minutes until the chicken is fully cooked. The capsicums should be softened.
2. Portion the soup into four bowls and top each with ¼ cup (32 g) cheese, 2 avocado slices and cilantro. Serve

immediately. The soup may be stored for 3 days in the fridge or up to a month in the freezer. Omit the avocado in this step.

Nutritional Facts: Cal: 602; Carb: 8g; Protein: 31.4g; Fat: 44.6g; Fiber: 13g; Sugars: 5g; Cholesterol: 83mg; Sodium: 805mg

5.5 Chicken Laksa

Serves: 4 Prep Time: 5 minutes Cook Time: 25 minutes

Ingredients:

- Coconut Oil, 1/3 cup (75 ml)
- White Onions, ¼ cup (32 g), peeled and diced
- Lemongrass, 4 stalks, cut lengthwise and crushed with the back of a knife
- Green Chili Pepper, 1 piece, seeded and diced
- Ginger, 1 2-inch piece, peeled and grated
- Garlic, 4 cloves, peeled and minced
- Coriander Seed, ground, 2 teaspoons (10 ml)
- Curry Powder, 2 teaspoons (10 ml)
- Dried Cumin Seed, 1 teaspoon (5ml), ground
- Salt
- Chicken Thighs, 1 pound (0.45 kg), boneless, skinless and sliced
- Coconut Milk, 1 (13.5 oz.) can
- Chicken Stock, 2 cups (475 ml)
- Bean Sprouts, 8 oz. (0.23 kg), washed and trimmed of wilted ends
- Lime Wedges
- Mint Leaves, 8 pieces

Procedure:

1. Heat the coconut oil in a saucepan over a medium setting. Sauté the onions, lemongrass, chili, ginger and garlic to form the base of the soup. Add the ground coriander seed, curry powder and cumin and season with salt. Cook for 10 minutes until aromatic.

2. Add the sliced chicken thighs, coconut milk and chicken stock. Bring the soup to a boil on high heat and reduce the heat to low. Allow this to simmer for 15 minutes or until chicken is fully cooked.

3. Remove the lemongrass. Portion the soup into four bowls and garnish with 2 oz. of bean sprouts, a lime wedge and 2 mint leaves. Serve immediately.

Nutritional Facts: Cal: 480; Carb: 8.3g; Protein: 37.3g; Fat: 32.9g; Fiber: 0.6g; Sugars: 0.7g; Cholesterol: 101mg; Sodium: 745mg

5.6 Unconventional Beef Curry

Serves: 4 Prep Time: 10 minutes Cook Time: 30 minutes

Ingredients:

- Coconut Oil, ½ cup (118 ml)
- Apple, 1 small piece, peeled, cored and diced
- Yellow Onion, 1 small piece, peeled and sliced
- Garlic, 2 cloves, peeled and minced
- Ginger, 1 3-inch piece, peeled and grated
- Curry Powder, 2 tablespoons (30 ml)
- Garam Masala, 2 teaspoons (10 ml)
- Boneless Beef Chuck Roast, 1 pound (0.45 kg), cubed into ¾ inch pieces
- Butternut Squash, 1 small piece, cubed
- Beef Stock, 1 cup (237 ml)
- Coconut Aminos, 1 tablespoon (15 ml)

Procedure:

1. Heat the coconut oil in a large saucepan over a medium setting. Sauté the apple, onion, garlic, ginger, curry powder and garam masala. Stir to coat the apples and onions with the spices and cook for 10 minutes until fragrant.

2. Add the beef, squash, stock, and coconut aminos. Cover the pot and bring the curry to a boil over high heat. Reduce the heat to medium low and simmer for 20 minutes until the squash has softened and the beef is tender.

3. Portion into 4 bowls and serve immediately.

Nutritional Facts: Cal: 698; Carb: 13.4g; Protein: 31.8g; Fat: 56g; Fiber: 3.5g; Sugars: 5.8g; Cholesterol: 118mg; Sodium: 82mg

5.7 Traditional Chicken Soup

Serves: 5 Prep Time: 10 minutes Cook Time: 55 minutes

Ingredients:

- Roasted Chicken, 1 whole, shredded, reserve the bones and offcuts.
- Water, 6 cups (1419.5 ml)
- Butter, 2 tablespoons (30 ml)
- Celery, 2 medium stalks
- Onion, ½ medium piece, peeled and chopped
- Bay Leaf, 1 piece
- Salt
- Black Pepper, freshly ground
- Cilantro Leaves, 1 tablespoon (15 ml), chopped
- Napa Cabbage, 2 cups (400 g) (64 g)sliced into strips

Procedure:

1. Cook the bones and offcuts of the chicken in water in a saucepan for 15 minutes over a medium high flame. Reduce the heat and allow the mixture to simmer for another 15 minutes.
2. Liquefy the butter in a large saucepan over a medium setting and sauté the onions and celery until softened and aromatic. Add the bay leaf, salt and pepper and pour in the broth. Let simmer for 10 minutes.
3. Once the soup is cooked, add the shredded chicken meat, cilantro and cabbage. Let simmer for 10 more minutes until the cabbage is softened. Portion into 5 bowls and serve.

Nutritional Facts: Cal: 265; Carb: 1.7g; Protein: 9.3g; Fat: 4.3g; Fiber: 1.7g; Sugars: 2.3g; Cholesterol: 38mg; Sodium: 136mg

5.8 Filipino Pork Soup

Serves: 4 Prep Time: 10 minutes Cook Time: 45 minutes

Ingredients:

- Butter, 1 teaspoon (5ml)
- Pork Ribs, boneless and chopped, 1 pound (0.45 kg)
- Shallot, 1 piece, peeled and minced
- Garlic, 2 cloves, minced
- Ginger, ½ inch piece, sliced
- Water, 1 cup (237 ml)
- Chicken Stock, 2 cups (475 ml)
- Fish Sauce, 1 tablespoon (15 ml)
- Cauliflower Rice, 1 cup (237 ml)
- Salt
- Black Pepper, freshly ground

Procedure:

1. Heat the butter in a medium saucepan over a medium high flame. Sear the pork ribs on all sides for 5 to 6 minutes. Add the shallots, garlic and ginger and sauté for 3 minutes until aromatic. Add the remainder of the ingredients and adjust seasonings to taste. Cover and allow to cook for 30 to 35 minutes until pork is tender. Portion into 4 bowls and serve.

Nutritional Facts: Cal: 203; Carb: 3.7g; Protein: 27.1g; Fat: 8.4g; Fiber: 1.1g; Sugars: 1.7g; Cholesterol: 277mg; Sodium: 696mg

5.9 Classic Tomato Soup

Serves: 4 Prep Time: 10 minutes Cook Time: 15 minutes

Ingredients:

- Tomato Paste, 12 oz.,
- Coconut Cream, 1 cup (237 ml)
- Water, ¼ cup (32 g)
- Cheddar Cheese, 1 cup (237 ml), shredded
- Oregano Leaves, dried, 1 teaspoon (5ml)
- Garlic, 1 clove, peeled and minced
- Salt
- Black Pepper

Procedure:

1. Add the tomato paste and coconut cream into a pot. Stir to combine and add the remainder of the ingredients except the cheese. Heat the mixture until it begins to simmer, allow to cook for 10 minutes.
2. Add the cheese and stir until liquefied. Cook for 5 more minutes. Portion into 4 bowls and serve immediately.

Nutritional Facts: Cal: 231; Carb: 11g; Protein: 8g; Fat: 4g; Fiber: 4g; Sugars: 12.5g; Cholesterol: 30mg; Sodium: 307mg

5.10 Spicy Poblano Soup

Serves: 6 Prep Time: 10 minutes Cook Time: 1 hour

Ingredients:

- Poblano Peppers, 10 pieces
- Ghee, 1 tablespoon (15 ml)
- Yellow Onion, 1 large piece, peeled and chopped
- Garlic, 4 cloves, peeled and minced
- Cilantro Leaves, 1 cup (237 ml), chopped
- Salt
- Black Pepper
- Vegetable Stock, 5 cups (1183 ml)
- Dried Cumin Seed, 1 teaspoon (5ml), ground
- Oaxaca Cheese, 14 oz., grated

Procedure:

1. Heat up an oven to 450 degrees Fahrenheit. Prepare a baking sheet and arrange the peppers on it. Roast them in the oven for 20 minutes and allow to cool. Peel the peppers, and chop.
2. Heat the ghee in a pot over a medium setting and sauté the onion and garlic. Add the cilantro, cumin, salt and pepper, and chopped peppers and cook for 6 minutes. Pour in the stock and cook for 20 minutes. Stir every few minutes.
3. Add the cheese. Use an immersion blender or pour the soup into a blender and puree until smooth. Portion into bowls and serve immediately.

Nutritional Facts: Cal: 261; Carb: 11g; Protein: 6g; Fat: 4g; Fiber: 7g; Sugars: 7.5g; Cholesterol: 5mg; Sodium: 952mg

5.11 Egg Drop Soup

Serves: 6 Prep Time: 10 minutes Cook Time: 40 minutes

Ingredients

- Chicken Stock, 6 cups (1419.5 ml)
- Coconut Aminos, 1 tablespoon (15 ml)
- Garlic, 2 cloves, crushed
- Ginger, 1 1-inch piece, peeled
- Scallions, 3 stalks, peeled and chopped
- Arrowroot Starch, 2 teaspoons (10 ml)
- Eggs, 3 large
- Egg Yolks, 2 pieces

Procedure:

1. Add the stock, aminos, garlic, ginger and scallions into a large stockpot and heat over a medium high flame. Bring to a boil and lower the heat to medium. Let simmer for 10 minutes. Remove the garlic, ginger and scallions and set aside.
2. Get some of the broth into a bowl and whisk in the arrowroot starch to form a slurry. Whisk until well incorporated and pour this back into the simmering broth. Stir for 5 minutes until the soup thickens.
3. In a separate bowl, add the eggs and egg yolks and lightly whisk. Pour this into the broth and allow to disperse for a minute. Remove from heat and let cool for a bit. Serve immediately into 6 bowls or store for up to a week in the fridge in an airtight container.

Nutritional Facts: Cal: 94; Carb: 3.5g; Protein: 9g; Fat: 5g; Fiber: 0g; Sugars: 0.5g; Cholesterol: 69mg; Sodium: 257mg

5.12 Cream of Mushroom Soup

Serves: 6 Prep Time: 10 minutes Cook Time: 25 minutes

Ingredients:

- Baby Portobello Mushrooms, 5 cups (1182.9 g), brushed and trimmed of stems
- Chicken Stock, 1 ½ cups (350 ml)
- Yellow Onion, ½ piece, peeled and chopped
- Thyme Leaves, ¼ teaspoon (1.25 ml) dried
- Butter, 3 tablespoons (45 ml)
- Coconut Flour, 3 tablespoons (45 ml)
- Arrowroot Starch, ½ teaspoon (2.5 ml)
- Salt
- Black Pepper, freshly ground
- Heavy Cream, 1 cup (237 ml)

Procedure:

1. Add the mushrooms, stock, onion and thyme leaves into a large stockpot and stir until well incorporated. Cook until the mushrooms have been softened, for 15 minutes. Pour the soup into a blender or use an immersion blender to puree until smooth. Set aside.
2. Make a roux by heating up the butter in a large saucepan and stirring in the coconut flour and arrowroot. Pour the pureed soup and season with the salt and pepper. Stir in the heavy cream. Bring the soup into a boil and stir constantly.
3. Remove from heat and let cool a bit before serving. You may store this for up to a week.

Nutritional Facts: Cal: 226; Carb: 4.5g; Protein: 4g; Fat: 21g; Fiber: 3.5g; Sugars: 3.5g; Cholesterol: 70mg; Sodium: 137mg

6 VEGETARIAN OPTIONS

6.1 Southwestern Stuffed Capsicums

Serves: 3 Prep Time: 10 minutes Cook Time: 45 minutes

Ingredients:

- Capsicums, 3 pieces, seeded and halved lengthwise
- Eggs, 3 medium, whisked
- Mexican Cheese Blend, 1 cup (237 ml)
- Chili Powder, 1 teaspoon (5ml)
- Garlic, 1 clove, peeled and minced
- Onion Powder, 1 teaspoon (5ml)
- Tomato, 1 large piece, chopped
- Mustard Powder, 1 teaspoon (5ml)

Procedure:

1. Heat up an oven to 350 degrees Fahrenheit. Spray a cookie sheet with some non-stick spray or vegetable oil.
2. Mix the eggs, chili powder, cheese blend, garlic, and onion powder. Portion this mixture in the halved capsicums. Mix the tomato and mustard powder and use to top the capsicums.
3. Cover with foil and bake for 45 minutes or until the peppers are softened and the filling is heated up. Serve immediately.

Nutritional Facts: Cal: 194; Carb: 3.5g; Protein: 13.3g; Fat: 13.9g; Fiber: 0.7g; Sugars: 2.4g; Cholesterol: 172mg; Sodium: 144mg

6.2 Greek Asparagus Frittata

Serves: 4 Prep Time: 10 minutes Cook Time: 25 minutes

Ingredients:

- Olive Oil, 1 tablespoon (15 ml)
- Red Onion, ½ piece, sliced
- Asparagus, 4 oz. (0.11 kg)cut into chunks
- Tomato, 1 piece, seeded and chopped
- Eggs, 5 whole, beaten
- Halloumi Cheese (you may omit this), 10 oz., crumbled
- Green Olives, 2 tablespoons (30 ml), pitted and sliced
- Parsley Leaves, fresh, 1 tablespoon (15 ml), chopped

Procedure:

1. Heat up an oven to 350 degrees Fahrenheit. Grease a baking pan with olive oil and set aside.
2. Heat olive oil in a pan over a medium high flame. Sauté the onion and asparagus for 3 minutes, stirring. Add the tomato and cook for 2 more minutes. Transfer the cooked vegetables into the prepared baking pan. Set aside.
3. Whisk the eggs and crumbled halloumi together and pour over the prepared vegetables. Place the sliced olives on top of the egg mixture. Bake for 15 minutes. Garnish with parsley and serve warm.

Nutritional Facts: Cal: 376; Carb: 4g; Protein: 24.5g; Fat: 29.1g; Fiber: 1g; Sugars: 2.5g; Cholesterol: 288mg; Sodium: 645mg

6.3 Avocado Baked Eggs

Serves: 4 Prep Time: 10 minutes Cook Time: 20 minutes

Ingredients:

- Avocadoes, 2, pitted and halved lengthwise.
- Eggs, 4 whole
- Salt
- Black Pepper, freshly ground
- Asiago Cheese, 1 cup (237 ml)
- Red Pepper Flakes, ½ teaspoon (2.5 ml)
- Rosemary Leaves, dried, ½ teaspoon (2.5 ml)
- Chives, 1 tablespoon (15 ml), finely chopped

Procedure:

1. Heat up oven to 420 degrees Fahrenheit. Line a baking tray with greaseproof paper and set aside.
2. Crack the eggs whole into the halved avocadoes. Be sure to keep the yolks intact. Season each egg with salt and pepper. Top with the cheese, red pepper flakes and rosemary leaves. Bake in the Heated oven for 15 minutes or until the eggs have set. Garnish with chives and serve immediately.

Nutritional Facts: Cal: 300; Carb: 5.4g; Protein: 14.9g; Fat: 24.6g; Fiber: 4.6g; Sugars: 0.5g; Cholesterol: 236mg; Sodium: 789mg

6.4 Zucchini au Gratin

Serves: 5 Prep Time: 10 minutes Cook Time: 50 minutes

Ingredients:

- Eggs, 10 large
- Yogurt, 3 tablespoons (45 ml)
- Zucchini, 2 large pieces, sliced
- Leek, ½ medium stalk, rinsed and sliced thinly
- Salt
- Black Pepper, freshly ground
- Cayenne Pepper, 1 teaspoon (5ml)
- Cream Cheese, 1 cup (237 ml)
- Garlic, 2 cloves, minced
- Swiss Cheese, 1 cup (237 ml), grated

Procedure:

1. Heat up an oven to 360 degrees Fahrenheit. Spray a non-stick baking pan with Cook spray. Set aside.
2. In a bowl, whisk the yogurt and eggs together. Place aside. Layer the leeks and zucchini in the prepared baking pan, then season with cayenne pepper and salt. Add the minced garlic and cream cheese. Add additional leeks and zucchini on top. Add the egg mixture last, then the Swiss cheese.
3. Bake for 40 minutes or until the top is golden. Serve immediately.

Nutritional Facts: Cal: 371; Carb: 5.2g; Protein: 15.7g; Fat: 32g; Fiber: 0.3g; Sugars: 2.6g; Cholesterol: 447mg; Sodium: 411mg

6.5 Mediterranean Vegetable Soup

Serves: 3 Prep Time: 10 minutes Cook Time: 30 minutes

Ingredients:

- Broccoli, 4 oz. (0.11 kg)
- Sesame Oil, 2 tablespoons (30 ml)
- Onion, 1 small piece, peeled and chopped
- Garlic, 2 cloves, minced
- Cayenne Pepper, 1 teaspoon (5ml)
- Salt
- Black Pepper, freshly ground
- Spinach Leaves, 1 cup (237 ml), shredded
- Celery, 1 medium stalk, chopped
- Vegetable Stock, 2 cups (475 ml)
- Water, 1 cup (237 ml)
- Tomato Puree, ½ cup
- Jalapeno Pepper, 1 piece, minced
- Italian Herb Mix, 1 tablespoon (15 ml)

Procedure:

1. Place the broccoli florets into the food processor and pulse until they are riced. Do this in batches and set aside.
2. Sesame oil is heated in a skillet on a medium heat setting. Garlic and onions should be sautéed until fragrant. After adding, simmer the riced broccoli for 2 minutes. The remaining ingredients—all but the spinach leaves—should be added.
3. Bring the soup to a boil over a medium high flame. Once it boils, reduce the heat to a medium low and allow to simmer, covered for about 25 minutes. Stir in the spinach leaves and switch off the heat. Keep covered to let the spinach wilt.
4. Portion into bowls and serve immediately.

Nutritional Facts: Cal: 137; Carb: 5.6g; Protein: 5.6g; Fat: 10.7g; Fiber: 1.2g; Sugars: 2.4g; Cholesterol: 0mg; Sodium: 585mg

6.6 Baked Creamed Kale

Serves: 4 Prep Time: 10 minutes Cook Time: 30 minutes

Ingredients:

- Cook Spray, 1 second
- Kale, 6 oz., midrib removed and leaves torn
- Eggs, 4, whisked
- Cheddar Cheese, 1 cup (237 ml), shredded
- Romano Cheese, 1 cup (237 ml),
- Sour Cream, 2 tablespoons (30 ml)
- Garlic, 1 clove, peeled and minced
- Salt
- Black Pepper, freshly ground
- Cayenne Pepper, ½ teaspoon (2.5 ml)

Procedure:

1. Heat up an oven to 365 degrees Fahrenheit. Spray a non-stick baking tray with the Cook spray and set aside. In a bowl, mix all of the ingredients and pour into the prepared baking tray. Bake for 30-35 minutes or until set. Serve immediately.

Nutritional Facts: Cal: 384; Carb: 5.9g; Protein: 25.1g; Fat: 29.1g; Fiber: 1.5g; Sugars: 1.8g; Cholesterol: 277mg; Sodium: 1004mg

6.7 Zucchini and Spinach Chowder

Serves: 4 Prep Time: 10 minutes Cook Time: 25 minutes

Ingredients:

- Garlic, 1 clove, peeled and minced
- Scallions, ½ cup, chopped
- Water, 4 cups
- Zucchini, 2 cups (400 g)sliced
- Celery, 1 medium stalk, chopped
- Vegetable Stock Cubes, 2 pieces
- Baby Spinach Leaves, 4 oz.,
- Salt
- Black Pepper, freshly ground
- Parsley Leaves, fresh, 1 tablespoon (15 ml)
- Butter, 1 tablespoon (15 ml)
- Olive Oil, 1 tablespoon (15 ml)
- Egg, 1 large, beaten

Procedure:

1. Garlic and scallions are sautéed in oil in a stockpot over a medium-high heat for 4 minutes, or until tender. Cook for 13 minutes after adding the vegetable stock cubes celery, zucchini, and water. Add the salt & pepper (to taste) and spinach leaves. Cook for another five minutes after adding the butter and parsley. Add the beaten egg and mix it in thoroughly. Fill bowls with the portion, then serve right away.

Nutritional Facts: Cal: 85; Carb: 3.8g; Protein: 3.7g; Fat: 5.9g; Fiber: 1.3g; Sugars: 1.2g; Cholesterol: 49mg; Sodium: 126mg

6.8 Mushroom Burgers

Serves; 6 Prep Time: 10 minutes Cook Time: 25 minutes

Ingredients:

- Ground Flaxseed, 1 tablespoon (15 ml)
- Water, 3 tablespoons (45 ml)
- Coconut Oil, 2 tablespoons (30 ml) divided into 1 tablespoon (15 ml)
- Portobello Mushrooms, fresh, 1 pound (0.45 kg), finely chopped
- Yellow Onion, 1 large, peeled and minced
- Garlic, 3 cloves, peeled and minced
- Coconut Aminos, 2 tablespoons (30 ml)
- Salt
- Black Pepper, freshly ground

Procedure:

1. In a small bowl, mix the flaxseed and water and allow to sit for 15 minutes until a gel forms.
2. Heat the coconut oil in a skillet over a medium setting and add the mushrooms, onions and garlic. Cook for four minutes and season with the Coconut Aminos. Cook for a minute more and remove from pan. Allow to cool.
3. This should be added to the food processor jar and pulsed until crushed. Season with salt and pepper and add the flaxseed mixture. Reset the pulse. Remove the food processor's blade, and stir thoroughly.
4. Form the mixture into six uniform patties, then fry them in a skillet with additional coconut oil. Cook until both sides are browned, turning once. Remove from heat and serve, or refrigerate in an airtight container for up to one week.

Nutritional Facts: Cal: 74; Carb: 4g; Protein: 2g; Fat: 5g; Fiber: 2g; Sugars: 3g; Cholesterol: 0mg; Sodium: 395mg

6.9 Broccoli Slaw

Serves: 6 Prep Time: 10 minutes Cook Time: 0 minutes

Ingredients:

- Coconut Oil Mayonnaise, 1/3 cup (75 ml)
- Cider Vinegar, 1 tablespoon (15 ml)
- Granulated Erythritol. 1 teaspoon (5ml)
- Lime Juice, 2 tablespoons (30 ml)
- Salt
- Black Pepper, freshly ground
- Broccoli Slaw, 2 (12 oz.) bags
- Onion, 1 small red, peeled and sliced

Procedure:

1. In a large bowl, combine the mayonnaise, vinegar, erythritol, lime juice, salt, and pepper. Toss in the slaw and onion to coat evenly. This can be served immediately or stored in the refrigerator for up to one week.

Nutritional Facts: Cal: 132; Carb: 7g; Protein: 3.5g; Fat: 10g; Fiber: 3g; Sugars: 2.5g; Cholesterol: 5mg; Sodium: 302mg

6.10 Greek Vegetable Bowl

Serves: 6 Prep Time: 15 minutes Cook Time: 15 minutes

Ingredients:

- Coconut Yogurt, 6 oz.,
- Spanish Paprika, 1 teaspoon (5ml)
- Garlic Powder, 1 teaspoon (5ml)
- Lime Juice, 3 teaspoons
- Coconut Oil, 2 teaspoons (10 ml)
- Cauliflower Rice, 3 cups (360 g)
- Tomatoes, 1 ½ cups (350 ml), diced
- Zucchini, 1 ½ cups (350 ml), diced
- Scallions, 6 stalks, chopped
- Cilantro Leaves, 6 tablespoons (90 ml), chopped
- Avocadoes, 2 large, pitted, halved and diced

Procedure:

1. Combine the coconut yogurt, Spanish paprika, garlic powder and lime juice in a small bowl and mix well. Set aside.
2. In a skillet heated to medium heat, sauté the cauliflower rice for three minutes, or until softened. Cook the tomatoes and zucchini for an additional 2 minutes. Remove the pan from heat and stir in the cilantro and scallions.
3. Portion the cauliflower rice into 6 bowls and top with the coconut yogurt. Place a bit of the diced avocado on top of the portions and serve or store, but omit the avocadoes.

Nutritional Facts: Cal: 171; Carb: 6g; Protein: 5g; Fat: 13g; Fiber: 7g; Sugars: 5g; Cholesterol: 7mg; Sodium: 41mg

6.11 Shirataki Spinach Noodles

Serves: 6 Prep Time: 10 minutes Cook Time: 15 minutes

Ingredients:

- Coconut Oil, 1 tablespoon (15 ml)
- Garlic, 2 cloves, peeled and minced
- Yellow Onion, 1 small, peeled and diced
- Frozen Spinach, 2 cups (400 g), thawed, drained and chopped
- Cream Cheese, 6 oz.,
- Vegan Parmesan Cheese, ¼ cup (32 g), grated
- Salt
- Black Pepper, freshly ground
- Shirataki Noodles, 2 (7 oz.,) packages, rinsed thoroughly

Procedure:

1. In a skillet, heat the coconut oil over medium heat. For four minutes, sauté the garlic and onion until tender and fragrant. Add the spinach and simmer for about 2 minutes, or until heated through. Incorporate the cream cheese, vegan Parmesan, pepper, and salt. Stir to get a uniform mixture.
2. Add the shirataki noodles and toss to coat in the mixture. Remove from heat and portion into 6 bowls. Serve immediately or store in the refrigerator for up to a week.

Nutritional Facts: Cal: 236; Carb: 6.5g; Protein: 10g; Fat: 13g; Fiber: 1.5g; Sugars: 1.5g; Cholesterol: 31mg; Sodium: 592mg

6.12 Egg Roll in a Bowl

Serves: 6 Prep Time: 10 minutes Cook Time: 15 minutes

Ingredients:

- Coconut Oil, 2 tablespoons (30 ml)
- Onion, 1 large red, peeled and sliced
- Broccoli Slaw, 1 cup (237 ml)
- Celery, 8 medium stalks, chopped
- Cabbage, 12 cups (2880g), shredded
- Button Mushrooms, 1 ½ cups (350 ml), brushed and sliced thinly
- Coconut Aminos, 1/3 cup (75 ml)
- Salt
- Black Pepper, freshly ground
- Water, 1 tablespoon (15 ml)
- Toasted Sesame Oil, 1 tablespoon (15 ml)
- Scallions, 1 tablespoon (15 ml), chopped
- Sesame Seeds, 2 tablespoons (30 ml)

Procedure:

1. In a skillet, heat the coconut oil over medium heat and sauté the onion for 5 minutes, or until tender. Season the pepper, salt, and mushrooms with coconut aminos, cabbage, celery, and broccoli. Sprinkle with water and simmer the vegetables for 10 minutes, or until tender.
2. Remove from the heat and sprinkle with the toasted sesame oil, scallions and sesame seeds. Let cool before you portion it into 6 bowls or airtight containers. Serve immediately or store in the fridge for up to a week.

Nutritional Facts: Cal: 162; Carb: 11g; Protein: 5g; Fat: 8.5g; Fiber: 8g; Sugars: 9g; Cholesterol: 0mg; Sodium: 398mg

6.13 Cheesy Pesto "Pasta" Bowl

Serves: 6 Prep Time: 10 minutes Cook Time: 20 minutes

Ingredients:

- Mascarpone Cheese, 12 oz.,
- Black Pepper, freshly ground
- Nutmeg, 1/8 teaspoon (0.6g), freshly grated
- Salt
- Pesto, ½ cup
- Zucchini Noodles, 8 cups, raw
- Asiago Cheese, ¼ cup (32 g), grated
- Broccoli Florets, ¾ cup (175 ml), steamed
- Vegan Parmesan Cheese, ½ cup, shredded
- Mozzarella Cheese, 1 ½ cups (350 ml), grated

Procedure:

1. Heat up an oven to 400 degrees Fahrenheit. Prepare a 9" by 13"baking tray and set aside.
2. In a saucepan, stir together the Mascarpone, Vegan Parmesan, Asiago, Salt, Pepper, Nutmeg and Pesto. Stir until the cheeses have liquefied together. Add the zucchini noodles and stir to coat for at least 2 minutes. Remove from the heat and transfer into the prepared baking tray.
3. Evenly arrange the broccoli florets in a single layer and sprinkle the mozzarella cheese on top. Bake in the heated oven for 10 minutes or until the cheese is bubbly. Remove from oven and cool.
4. Portion this into six even portions and serve immediately or store each portion separately in an airtight container in the fridge for up to a week.

Nutritional Facts: Cal: 429; Carb: 8g; Protein: 17g; Fat: 36g; Fiber: 3g; Sugars: 6.5g; Cholesterol: 28mg; Sodium: 773mg

6.14 Vegetarian Fajitas

Serves: 6 Prep Time: 10 minutes Cook Time: 15 minutes

Ingredients:

- Black Pepper, freshly ground
- Garlic, 2 cloves, peeled and minced
- Green Capsicums, 2 medium sized, seeded and julienned
- Salt
- Red Capsicums, 2 medium sized, seeded and julienned
- Yellow Capsicum, 1 medium sized, seeded and julienned
- Onion, 1 medium, red, peeled and thinly sliced
- Portobello Mushrooms, 1 cup (237 ml), sliced
- Garlic Powder, ½ teaspoon (2.5 ml)
- Scallions, 3 cups (360 g), sliced
- Green Chiles, 1 (4 oz.) can
- Chili Powder, 1 teaspoon (5ml)
- Dried Cumin Seed, 1 teaspoon (5ml), ground
- Coconut Oil, 1 tablespoon (15 ml)

Procedure:

1. In a large skillet, heat the coconut oil over medium heat and sauté the garlic for one minute. Add the peppers and simmer for two minutes, or until they have softened. Add the onions and sauté for an additional 2 minutes, until they have softened. Cover the skillet with the lid after adding the mushrooms, scallions, chilies, and the other seasonings. Cook the vegetables for at least 5 minutes, or until they are tender.
2. Remove from the heat and let cool. Portion into six equal portions and serve or store in airtight containers in the fridge for up to a week.

Nutritional Facts: Cal: 68; Carb: 7g; Protein: 2g; Fat: 2.5g; Fiber: 3g; Sugars: 5g; Cholesterol: 0mg; Sodium: 215mg

7 BEEF, PORK AND LAMB DISHES

7.1 Keto Sausages and Peppers

Serves: 4 Prep Time: 5 minutes Cook Time: 20 minutes

Ingredients:

- Green Capsicum, 1 small, thinly sliced
- Red Capsicum, 1 small, thinly sliced
- Garlic Powder, 1 ½ teaspoons (5.9 g)
- Oregano Leaves, dried, 1 teaspoon (5ml)
- Smoked Sausages, 12 oz., sliced thinly
- Spanish Paprika, 1 teaspoon (5ml)
- Salt
- Black Pepper, freshly ground
- Coconut Oil, ¼ cup (32 g)
- Parsley Leaves, fresh, ¼ cup (32 g), chopped

Procedure:

1. Heat the oil in a medium skillet over a medium-low flame until it begins to shimmer. Once it shimmers, add all of the ingredients except for the parsley. Cover with a lid and cook for 15 minutes until the capsicums are softened. Remove the lid and continue to cook for 5-6 minutes until the liquid evaporates. Remove from heat and sprinkle with parsley. Serve immediately.

Nutritional Facts: Cal: 411; Carb: 4.8g; Protein: 11.1g; Fat: 38.3g; Fiber: 1.5g; Sugars: 1.9g; Cholesterol: 49mg; Sodium: 903mg

7.2 Steak Salad Cups

Serves: 6 Prep Time: 10 minutes plus 2 hours to marinate Cook Time: 8 minutes

Ingredients:

- Avocado Oil, ¼ cup (32 g) plus 2 tablespoons (30 ml)
- Coconut Aminos, ¼ cup (32 g)
- Hot Sauce, 2 tablespoons (30 ml)
- Lime Juice, 2 tablespoons (30 ml)
- Garlic, 6 cloves, peeled and minced
- Black Pepper, freshly ground
- Sirloin Steak, 1 pound (0.45 kg), cubed
- Red Onion, 1 whole, peeled and diced
- Yellow Capsicum, 1 whole, seeded and julienned
- Endive Leaves, 36 pieces or about 6 heads. \
- Parsley Leaves, ¼ cup (32 g), fresh, chopped

Procedure:

1. Make the marinade first. Combine the avocado oil, coconut aminos, hot sauce, lime juice, garlic and pepper in a bowl. Whisk to combine and add the cubed steak, onion and capsicums. Cover and chill for 2 hours to marinate, or overnight for better results.
2. Once the steak has marinated, transfer the contents of the bowl to a large frying pan. Cook over a medium setting and stir the steak frequently, until fully cooked, for about 8 minutes.
3. Portion the endive leaves into six plates. Add two tablespoons of the steak mixture on each leaf. Sprinkle with parsley and serve.

Nutritional Facts: Cal: 325; Carb: 12.3g; Protein: 25.8g; Fat: 19.2g; Fiber: 6.2g; Sugars: 2.3g; Cholesterol: 68mg; Sodium: 229mg

7.3 Pasta-Free Lasagna Casserole

Serves: 6 Prep Time: 10 minutes Cook Time: 30 minutes

Ingredients:

- Rosemary Leaves, dried, ¼ teaspoon (1.25 ml)
- Red Pepper Flakes, ¼ teaspoon (1.25 ml)
- Onion Powder, ½ teaspoon (2.5 ml)
- Coconut Oil, 3 tablespoons (45 ml)
- Beef Mince, 1 pound (0.45 kg)
- Fire-Roasted Tomatoes, 1 (14.5 oz.) can, crushed
- Tomato Paste, 1 (6 oz.) can
- Cider Vinegar, 2 teaspoons (10 ml)
- Basil Leaves, dried, 2 teaspoons (10 ml)
- Garlic Powder, 1 teaspoon (5ml)
- Oregano Leaves, dried, 1 teaspoon (5ml)
- Bay Leaf, 1 large leaf
- Salt
- Thyme Leaves, dried, ¼ teaspoon (1.25 ml)

For the Cheese:

- Coconut Oil, ¼ cup (32 g)
- Parsley Leaves, fresh, ¼ cup (32 g), chopped to garnish
- Non-Dairy Milk, ¼ cup (32 g)
- Onion Powder, ½ teaspoon (2.5 ml)
- Nutritional Yeast, ¼ cup (32 g)
- Egg Yolks, 4 large
- Dijon Mustard, 1 teaspoon (5ml) (5ml)
- Lemon Juice, 1 teaspoon (5ml) (5ml)
- Garlic Powder, ½ teaspoon (2.5 ml)

Procedure:

1. In a large skillet, heat the oil over medium heat and cook the ground beef until no longer pink, about 6 minutes. Use a spatula to separate the meat clumps. Stir in the crushed thyme, rosemary, crushed red pepper, onion powder, salt, bay leaf, oregano, garlic powder, basil, vinegar, tomatoes and tomato paste. Cover and cook on low for fifteen minutes.
2. Make the cheese sauce: Add all of the ingredients into a bowl and whisk until smooth.
3. Once the meat sauce is cooked, remove the bay leaf and pat out the meat with a spatula into an even layer. Top with the cheese sauce. Cover and cook on low for 10 minutes or until the topping is cooked and no longer sticky. Portion into six bowls and garnish with parsley. Serve immediately,

Nutritional Facts: Cal: 507; Carb: 12.9g; Protein: 35.3g; Fat: 32.6g; Fiber: 5.2g; Sugars: 8.3g; Cholesterol: 249mg; Sodium: 545mg

7.4 Chimichurri Steak Sandwich

Serves: 4 Prep Time: 10 minutes Cook Time: 5 minutes

Ingredients:

- Eggs, 8 large
- Garlic Powder, ½ teaspoon (2.5 ml)
- Onion Powder, ½ teaspoon (2.5 ml)
- Salt
- Black Pepper, freshly ground
- Avocado Oil, 2 tablespoons (30 ml)
- Chimichurri, 1 cup (237 ml) divided into ½ cup portions
- Skirt Steak, 1 pound (0.45 kg), grilled and sliced thinly
- Mixed Greens, 4 cups

Procedure:

1. Crack the eggs into a bowl and season with the garlic powder, onion powder, salt and pepper. Whisk until well incorporated.
2. Add the avocado oil into a non-stick skillet. Obtain the lid rings of a Mason jar and line with oil. Arrange flat side down in the skillet and heat on medium low for a minute. Pour the egg into the rings, about ¼ cup (32 g) portions, or until the egg mixture reaches the rim. You may use an oiled ring mold if you have it.
3. Cover with a lid and cook for 5 minutes or until the eggs are set. Remove from heat and allow to sit for 2 minutes. Remove the eggs with a spatula and separate the eggs from the rings.
4. Spread the egg bun with a Chimichurri and layer the steak on top. Top with another egg bun. This should make 4 sandwiches. Serve with a cup of the salad greens topped with two tablespoons of Chimichurri.

Nutritional Facts: Cal: 593; Carb: 6.2g; Protein: 45.3g; Fat: 43g; Fiber: 1.9g; Sugars: 2.1g; Cholesterol: 435mg; Sodium: 411mg

7.5 Slow-Cooked Barbecue Beef with Slaw

Serves: 4 Prep Time: 10 minutes Cook Time: 45 minutes or 4-6 hours

Ingredients:

- Beef Chuck Roast, 1 pound (0.45 kg), boneless
- Beef Broth, 1 cup (237 ml)
- Salt
- Barbecue Sauce, ½ cup, sugar-free
- Coleslaw Mix, 9 oz.,
- Poppy-Seed Dressing, ½ cup, sugar-free

Procedure:

1. Arrange the chuck roast, salt and beef stock in a slow cooker or pressure cooker. If a pressure cooker is used, seal the pressure cooker and set the timer for 45 minutes on high pressure. Once the time has elapsed, release the pressure carefully before you remove the lid. If the slow cooker is used, cook on high for 4 hours or on low for 6 hours.
2. Drain the meat, but reserve ¼ cup (32 g) of the liquid from the cooker, once cooked. Shred the meat and toss with the barbecue sauce. In a salad bowl, toss the coleslaw mix with the poppy-seed dressing to coat. Arrange on a plate with the beef in even portions on 4 plates and serve immediately.

Nutritional Facts: Cal: 354; Carb: 4.6g; Protein: 23.9g; Fat: 26.7g; Fiber: 1.7g; Sugars: 2.5g; Cholesterol: 70mg; Sodium: 566mg

7.6 Crispy Pork with Zesty Cauliflower Rice

Serves: 4 Prep Time: 5 minutes Cook Time: 40 minutes

Ingredients:

- Coconut Oil, ¼ cup (32 g)
- Pork Rinds, ¼ cup (32 g), crushed
- Garlic Powder, 1 teaspoon (5ml) (5ml)
- Oregano Leaves, dried, 1 teaspoon (5ml) (5ml)
- Thyme Leaves, dried, 1 teaspoon (5ml) (5ml)
- Salt
- Black Pepper, freshly ground
- Boneless Pork Chops, 1 pound (0.45 kg), about 1 inch thick.
- Cauliflower, 1 medium head or Cauliflower Rice, 3 cups (360 g)
- Onion, 1 small white, peeled and diced
- Garlic, 4 cloves, peeled and minced
- Chicken Stock, ¼ cup (32 g)
- Lemon Juice, 2 tablespoons (30 ml)
- Salt
- Thyme Leaves, fresh, 6 sprigs

Procedure:

1. Heat the oil in a large pan over a medium setting. While the oil heats, stir together the crushed pork rinds, garlic powder, oregano, thyme leaves, salt and pepper in a wide bowl. Coat the pork chops one at a time in this mixture and fry, 10 minutes on each side until pork is seared.

2. If you are using prepared cauliflower rice, cook the cauliflower in the pan where the pork was cooked, together with the onion, garlic, chicken stock, lemon juice and salt. Cover and cook until the rice is softened, for about 15 minutes, stirring occasionally. If using a whole cauliflower, break the head into florets and pulse in the jar of a food processor until riced. Cook in the same steps as the prepared cauliflower rice.

3. Cut the pork chops into half-inch slices place into the pan where the rice was cooked. If the pork is uncooked, cook for 5 more minutes until done. Portion the pork and rice evenly among four plates and serve immediately,

Nutritional Facts: Cal: 419; Carb: 6g; Protein: 34g; Fat: 27.7g; Fiber: 3g; Sugars: 3g; Cholesterol: 104mg; Sodium: 728mg

7.7 Pork with Kale

Serves: 4 Prep Time: 5 minutes Cook Time: 35 minutes

Ingredients:

- Coconut Oil, 3 tablespoons (45 ml)
- Spanish Paprika, 1 teaspoon (5ml)
- Salt
- Black Pepper, freshly ground
- Boneless Pork Chops, 1 pound (0.45 kg), about an inch thick
- Onion, 1 small yellow, peeled and sliced
- Garlic, 6 cloves, peeled and minced
- Kale Leaves, 4 cups, midribs removed
- Creamy Italian Dressing, 1/3 cup (75 ml)
- Parsley Leaves, fresh, ¼ cup (32 g), chopped, to garnish

Procedure:

1. Heat the oil in a large pan over a medium setting. While the oil heats, mix in a wide bowl the Spanish paprika, salt and pepper. Coat the pork chops one at a time in the mix and cook in the pan, 10 minutes on each side until seared. Transfer onto a clean plate.
2. Add the onions and garlic into the pan where the pork was cooked and sauté for 5 minutes or until fragrant. Add the kale and dressing to the pan and cook until the kale is cooked but not wilted. Remove from the heat.
3. Cut pork into half-inch slices and if uncooked, add into the pan to cook for 5 more minutes. Otherwise, portion the pork and kale evenly onto 4 plates and garnish with parsley. Serve immediately.

Nutritional Facts: Cal: 429; Carb: 9.7g; Protein: 28g; Fat: 31g; Fiber: 3.1g; Sugars: 2.1g; Cholesterol: 77mg; Sodium: 432mg

7.8 Southwestern Cabbage and Bacon

Serves: 4 Prep Time: 10 minutes Cook Time: 25 minutes

Ingredients:

- Bacon, 6 strips, diced
- Red Onion, 1 small, peeled and diced
- Garlic, 4 cloves, minced
- Green Cabbage, 1 small head, cored and sliced thinly
- Fresh Chorizo, 12 oz., sliced thinly
- Beef Stock, ½ cup

Procedure:

1. Add the bacon, onion and garlic in a large pan and sauté over a medium setting until the bacon is crisped and onion and garlic are aromatic, about 10 minutes. Add the cabbage, sliced chorizo and beef stock. Cover with a lid and cook for 15 minutes until the cabbage and chorizo is cooked through.
2. Remove the lid and portion into 4 dinner plates.

Nutritional Facts: Cal: 523; Carb: 8g; Protein: 20g; Fat: 43.8g; Fiber: 4g; Sugars: 6g; Cholesterol: 93mg; Sodium: 980mg

7.9 Zucchini Pasta and Meatballs

Serves: 6 Prep Time: 10 minutes Cook Time: 20 minutes

Ingredients:

- Turkey Mince, 1 pound (0.45 kg)
- Pork Mince, 1 pound (0.45 kg)
- Mozzarella Cheese, dairy-free or regular, ½ cup, grated
- Hot Sauce, 2 tablespoons (30 ml)
- Oregano Leaves, dried, 2 teaspoons (10 ml)
- Basil Leaves, dried, 1 ½ teaspoons (5.9 g)
- Garlic Powder, 1 ¼ teaspoons
- Onion Powder, 1 teaspoon (5ml)
- Salt
- Rosemary Leaves, dried, ½ teaspoon (2.5 ml)
- Coconut Oil, 3 tablespoons (45 ml)
- Zucchinis, 4 medium, spiralized
- Lemon Juice, 1 tablespoon (15 ml)

Procedure:

1. Add the turkey, pork, cheese, hot sauce, oregano, basil, onion powder, garlic powder, salt and rosemary into a bowl and mix well.
2. Heat the oil in a large skillet over a medium setting. While the oil heats, shape the meatballs from the meat mixture, using about 3 tablespoons (45 ml) of the mixture per meatball. This should form about a dozen and a half meatballs. Add the meatballs into the pan and cover with a lid. Let cook for 15 minutes. Add the spiralized zucchini and lemon juice into the pan and cover. Let cook for 5 more minutes. Portion into 6 plates and serve immediately.

Nutritional Facts: Cal: 595; Carb: 2.6g; Protein: 43.8g; Fat: 45.2g; Fiber: 1g; Sugars: 0.9g; Cholesterol: 163mg; Sodium: 670mg

7.10 Pulled Pork Pasta

Serves: 6 Prep Time: 10 minutes Cook Time: 45 minutes or 4-6 hours

Ingredients:

- Pork Shoulder, 2 pounds, boneless
- Chicken Stock, 1 cup (237 ml)
- Salt
- Avocado Oil, 2 tablespoons (30 ml)
- Red Capsicum, 1 piece, seeded and diced
- Onion, 1 small white, peeled and diced
- Chestnut Mushrooms, 8 pieces, diced
- Pork Mince, 1 pound (0.45 kg)
- Barbecue Sauce, ¾ cup (175 ml), sugar-free
- Cook Liquid from Pork Shoulder, ½ cup

Procedure:

1. Add the pork shoulder, chicken stock and salt into a slow cooker or pressure cooker. If using a pressure cooker, seal the lid and cook on high pressure for 45 minutes. Allow the pressure to release carefully. Reserve half a cup of the Cook liquid and remove the meat. Keep ¼ cup (32 g) of the Cook liquid in the pressure cooker.
2. If using a slow cooker, cook on high for 4 hours or on low for 6 hours. Once the meat is cooked, reserve half a cup of the Cook liquid and remove the meat. Keep ¼ cup (32 g) of the Cook liquid in the slow cooker.
3. Heat the oil in a large pan over a medium setting and sauté the capsicums and onions until softened. Add the pork mince and cook for 5 minutes until no longer pink. Crumble any lumps with a spatula. Add the barbecue sauce and Cook liquid and stir. Cook for 3 more minutes to heat the sauce.
4. Shred the meat and portion into 6 plates. Top with the sauce and serve immediately.

Nutritional Facts: Cal: 683; Carb: 7.2g; Protein: 57.8g; Fat: 46g; Fiber: 1.8g; Sugars: 3.2g; Cholesterol: 211mg; Sodium: 768mg

7.11 Garlic-Baked Pork Chops

Serves: 6 Prep Time: 10 minutes Cook Time: 25 minutes

Ingredients:

- Butter, 3 tablespoons (45 ml), liquefied
- Eggs, 2 large, beaten
- Coconut Milk, 3 tablespoons (45 ml)
- Pork Chops, 6 4 oz. (0.11 kg)pieces, butterflied
- Granulated Garlic, 1 teaspoon (5ml)
- Garlic Salt, ¼ teaspoon (1.25 ml)

Procedure:

1. Heat up an oven to 425 degrees Fahrenheit and cover the bottom of a 9" by 13" inch baking tray with liquefied butter. Set aside.
2. Whisk the eggs and coconut milk together in a bowl. Dip the pork chops into the mix and sprinkle with the granulated garlic and season with the garlic salt. Arrange in the prepared baking tray.
3. Bake 10 minutes on one side, and 10 minutes on the other, until no longer pink, Remove from the oven and let cool. Serve or store in an airtight container for up to a week in the fridge.

Nutritional Facts: Cal: 234; Carb: 0.5g; Protein: 26g; Fat: 13g; Fiber: 0g; Sugars: 0g; Cholesterol: 390mg; Sodium: 188mg

7.12 Mediterranean Pulled Pork

Serves: 6 Prep Time: 10 minutes Cook Time: 8 hours, 30 minutes

Ingredients:

- Pork Tenderloin, 1 ½ pounds
- Greek Seasoning, 1 ½ tablespoons
- Pepperoncini Peppers, 1 (16 oz.) jar, sliced

Procedure:

1. Rub the pork tenderloin with the Greek Seasoning, Add the pork into the slow cooker, add the jar of the pepperoncini peppers including the liquid and cook on low for 8 hours. Remove the pork after 8 hours and shred. Return to the slow cooker and cook for 30 minutes. Remove from the heat and allow to cool. Portion into six and serve or store in an airtight container for up to a week.

Nutritional Facts: Cal: 151; Carb: 6g; Protein: 24g; Fat: 2.5g; Fiber: 1g; Sugars: 0g; Cholesterol: 260mg; Sodium: 64mg

8 SEAFOOD

8.1 Southern Shrimp Salad

Serves: 4 Prep Time: 5 minutes Cook Time: 15 minutes

Ingredients:

- Large Shrimp,, 1 pound (0.45 kg), peeled and deveined
- Avocado Oil, 2 tablespoons (30 ml)
- Garlic, 2 cloves, minced
- Basil Leaves, dried, 2 teaspoons (10 ml)
- Thyme Leaves, dried, 2 teaspoons (10 ml)
- Spanish Paprika, 1 ¾ teaspoons
- Black Pepper, freshly ground
- Salt
- Cayenne Pepper, 1/8 teaspoon (0.6g)
- Asparagus, 1 bunch with the woody ends snapped off, halved crosswise
- Butter Lettuce, 1 head, chopped
- Avocado, 1 medium piece, pitted, peeled and thinly sliced
- Onion, 1 red, small, peeled and thinly sliced
- Creamy Italian Dressing, ½ cup

Procedure:

1. In a large frying pan, add the shrimp, avocado oil, garlic, basil, thyme, Spanish paprika, salt and pepper. Toss to coat evenly. Heat the frying pan over a medium setting and cook the shrimp until pink, about 5 minutes.
2. Add the asparagus into the pan and cover with a lid. Cook for 10 minutes until tender.
3. Portion the lettuce, avocado and onion into four plates. Once the shrimp and asparagus are done Cook, transfer them into equal portions onto each plate. Top each plate with two tablespoons of dressing and toss. Serve immediately.

Nutritional Facts: Cal: 485; Carb: 12.2g; Protein: 32.2g; Fat: 31g; Fiber: 7.2g; Sugars: 5.4g; Cholesterol: 242mg; Sodium: 636mg

8.2 Glazed Salmon and Noodles

Serves: 4 Prep Time: 5 minutes Cook Time: 20 minutes

Ingredients:

- Avocado Oil, ¼ cup (32 g) plus 2 tablespoons (30 ml)
- Coconut Aminos, ¼ cup (32 g)
- Tomato Paste, 2 tablespoons (30 ml) plus 2 teaspoons (10 ml)
- Cider Vinegar, 2 tablespoons (30 ml)
- Ginger, 1 2-inch piece, peeled and grated
- Garlic, 4 cloves, minced
- Salt
- Salmon Fillets, 1 pound (0.45 kg), cut into 4 equal portions
- Konjac Noodles or other low-carb Noodles, 2 (7 oz.) packages
- Scallions, 2 stalks, sliced thinly
- Cilantro Leaves, 1 handful, chopped
- Sesame Seeds, 1 teaspoon (5ml)

Procedure:

1. In a skillet, heat two tablespoons of the avocado oil. While the oil heats, in a small bowl, whisk together the coconut aminos, tomato paste, vinegar, ginger, garlic and salt with the ¼ cup (32 g) Avocado oil.
2. Once the oil has heated up, add the salmon into the hot pan, skin side up. Reduce the heat to low and brush the salmon with the sauce to glaze it. Add the remainder of the sauce directly into the pan and cover the pan with a lid. Cook the salmon on low for 15 minutes until the salmon is seared and lightly cooked through.
3. Move the salmon to the side of the pan to make enough room for the noodles. In the pan where the salmon was cooked, toss the noodles and the scallions in the sauce. Add the cooked

salmon on top of the noodles and cook for 3 to 5 minutes, enough to heat the noodles.

4. Transfer onto 4 individual plates and garnish with the cilantro and sesame seeds. Drizzle the reduced pan sauce over the salmon and noodles and serve immediately.

Nutritional Facts: Cal: 333; Carb: 4.6g; Protein: 24.7g; Fat: 22.4g; Fiber: 3.6g; Sugars: 0.9g; Cholesterol: 45mg; Sodium: 287mg

8.3 Scallops in the Sea

Serves: 4 Prep Time: 5 minutes Cook Time: 35 minutes

Ingredients:

- Coconut Oil, ¼ cup (32 g)
- Broccoli Florets, 6 cups (1419.5 g),
- Garlic, 6 cloves, peeled and minced
- Ginger, 1 2-inch piece, peeled and grated
- Chicken Stock, 2/3 cup
- Mozzarella Cheese, dairy free or regular, ½ cup, shredded
- Sea Scallops, 1 pound (0.45 kg)
- Salt
- Black Pepper, freshly ground
- Coconut Oil, 2 tablespoons (30 ml)
- Lemon Wedges, for garnish

Procedure:

1. Prepare the broccoli mash first: In a large saucepan, heat the coconut oil and sauté the garlic, ginger, and broccoli, for around 5 minutes, until the garlic is fragrant. Pour the chicken stock into the pan and cover it with a lid. Cook the broccoli over low heat for 25 minutes, or until it can be mashed with a potato masher or fork.

2. Before the broccoli is done, pat the scallops dry and place them on a platter. On all sides, press salt and black pepper into the meat using your hands. In a skillet heated to medium temperature, lay the scallops. Cook scallops for two minutes per side, or until golden brown.

3. With a fork, mash the mozzarella cheese into the mashed broccoli. On four dishes, divide the mashed potatoes and arrange the scallops. Serve with lemon wedges as garnish.

Nutritional Facts: Cal: 353; Carb: 5g; Protein: 19.2g; Fat: 25.4g; Fiber: 7g; Sugars: 1g; Cholesterol: 27mg; Sodium: 768mg

8.4 Salmon and Sautéed Kale

Serves: 4 Prep Time: 5 minutes plus 2 hours to marinate Cook Time: 15 minutes

Ingredients:

- Salmon Fillets, 1 pound (0.45 kg), cut into four equal portions
- Vinaigrette, ¾ cup (175 ml)
- Onion, 1 small red, peeled and thinly sliced
- Kale Leaves, 4 cups, midrib removed and leaves rinsed
- Red Pepper Flakes, ¼ teaspoon (1.25 ml)
- Salt

Procedure:

1. Prepare a baking pan and lay the salmon fillets in it. Pour the vinaigrette on top of the salmon and allow to marinate for 2 hours in the refrigerator. Once the two hours have lapsed, transfer the salmon and the marinade into a skillet heated on a medium low flame. Arrange the onion slices around the fish and cook the salmon for 6 minutes on each side until seared.
2. Once the salmon has been cooked on both sides, push them to the side of the pan and add the kale. Season the kale with the red pepper flakes and salt. Toss to coat the leaves in the remnants of the marinade in the pan. Cover with a lid and cook for 3 minutes or until the kale has wilted.
3. Portion into 4 plates and serve immediately.

Nutritional Facts: Cal: 438; Carb: 5.8g; Protein: 26.3g; Fat: 33g; Fiber: 3.3g; Sugars: 3.8g; Cholesterol: 52mg; Sodium: 374mg

8.5 Salmon and Vegetable Noodles

Serves: 4 Prep Time: 5 minutes Cook Time: 35 minutes

Ingredients:

- Spanish Paprika, 1 teaspoon (5ml)
- Thyme Leaves, dried, 1 teaspoon (5ml)
- Basil Leaves, dried, ½ teaspoon (2.5 ml)
- Oregano Leaves, dried, ½ teaspoon (2.5 ml)
- Salt
- Black Pepper, freshly ground
- Salmon Fillets, 1 pound (0.45 kg) cut into 4 equal portions
- Tomatoes, 2 large, seeded and diced
- Chicken Stock, ½ cup
- Coconut Milk, ½ cup
- Garlic, 3 cloves, peeled and minced
- Red Pepper Flakes, ½ teaspoon (2.5 ml)
- Zucchinis, 2 medium, spiralized
- Coconut Oil 2 tablespoons (30 ml)
- Spinach, 1 cup (237 ml), chopped
- Bacon, 4 strips, cooked until crisp, crumbled
- Mozzarella Cheese, ¾ cup (175 ml), dairy-free or regular, shredded

Procedure:

1. Heat a large frying pan over a medium setting, while the oil heats up, in a wide bowl or dish, stir together the Spanish paprika, thyme, basil, oregano, salt and pepper. Coat the salmon in the herb and spice mix. Once all are coated in the spice mix, arrange them in the heated pan carefully and cook on 6 minutes on each side.
2. Once the salmon has been cooked, transfer onto a plate and set aside. Add the tomatoes, chicken stock, coconut milk, garlic and red pepper flakes and season with salt. Cook over a medium setting for 15 minutes, stirring

occasionally, until the sauce has thickened.

3. Add the spiralized zucchini and spinach into the sauce and stir to coat them evenly. Arrange the cooked salmon on top of the noodles and top with the bacon and cheese. Cover with a heat and cook on low for a few minutes or until the cheese has liquefied.

4. Portion into 4 plates and serve immediately.

Nutritional Facts: Cal: 485; Carb: 6g; Protein: 30g; Fat: 35g; Fiber: 6.5g; Sugars: 3g; Cholesterol: 71mg; Sodium: 829mg

8.6 Curried Shrimp

Serves: 4 Prep Time: 15 minutes Cook Time: 30 minutes

Ingredients:

- Coconut Oil, 1/3 cup (75 ml)
- Onion, 1 small white, peeled and sliced
- Fennel, 1 small bulb, sliced
- Red Curry Paste, 3 tablespoons (45 ml)
- Ginger Root, 1 2-inch piece, grated
- Salt
- Coconut Milk, 1 (13.5 oz.) can
- Shrimp, 1 pound (0.45 kg), peeled and deveined with their tails removed
- Cauliflower Rice, 2 cups (400 g)
- Cilantro Leaves, ½ cup

Procedure:

1. In a large saucepan, heat the oil over medium heat and cook the onions, fennel, curry paste, ginger, and salt for 10 minutes, or until fragrant. Transfer the curry paste mixture that has been sautéed to a blender or food processor. Blend the coconut milk until it is completely smooth.

2. Return the mixture into the saucepan and add the shrimp and cauliflower rice. Cover with a lid and bring the mix to a boil over a medium high flame. Once it begins to boil lightly, reduce to a medium low flame and allow to simmer for 20 minutes, until the cauliflower rice is softened. Portion into bowls and serve immediately.

Nutritional Facts: Cal: 499; Carb: 10.8g; Protein: 27.2g; Fat: 37.1g; Fiber: 3.4g; Sugars: 2.3g; Cholesterol: 222mg; Sodium: 1259mg

8.7 Hearty Shrimp and Vegetable Fry

Serves: 4 Prep Time: 5 minutes Cook Time: 20 minutes

Ingredients:

- Coconut Oil, ¼ cup (32 g)
- Medium Shrimp, 1 pound (0.45 kg), peeled, deveined with tails removed
- Smoked Sausage, 12 oz., cubed
- Asparagus, 5 spears, wooden ends trimmed, sliced thinly
- Chestnut Mushrooms, 4 oz. (0.11 kg)brushed and sliced
- Onion Powder, 1 teaspoon (5ml)
- Cayenne Pepper, 1/8 teaspoon (0.6g)
- Zucchini, 1 medium piece, peeled and cubed
- Black Pepper, freshly ground
- Spanish Paprika, 1 tablespoon (15 ml)
- Garlic Powder, 2 teaspoons (10 ml)
- Thyme Leaves, dried, 1 teaspoon (5ml)
- Salt
- Parsley Leaves, fresh, chopped, for garnish

Procedure:

1. Heat the Cook oil in a large skillet over a medium setting. Add all of the ingredients except for the parsley into the pan and toss to coat in the oil. Cover with a lid and allow to cook for 15-20 minutes or until the asparagus has softened, and the shrimp is pink. Portion into 4 plates and sprinkle with chopped parsley. Serve immediately.

Nutritional Facts: Cal: 574; Carb: 6.1g; Protein: 45g; Fat: 40.1g; Fiber: 2.3g; Sugars: 2.6g; Cholesterol: 311mg; Sodium: 1157mg

8.8 Swedish Seafood Salad

Serves: 3 Prep Time: 10 minutes Cook Time: 0 minutes

Ingredients:

- Pickled Herring, 6 pieces, drained and flaked with a fork
- Baby Spinach Leaves, ½ cup
- Salt
- Basil Leaves, fresh, 2 tablespoons (30 ml)
- Chives, fresh, 2 tablespoons (30 ml), chopped
- Garlic, 1 clove, peeled and minced
- Black Pepper, freshly ground
- Capsicum, 1 piece, seeded and chopped
- Onion, 1 small red, peeled and chopped
- Key Lime Juice, freshly squeezed

Procedure:

1. Combine the herring, spinach, basil, chives, garlic, capsicum and onion in a large bowl. Drizzle the key lime juice and season the salad with salt and pepper. Toss before serving.

Nutritional Facts: Cal: 134; Carb: 5.4g; Protein: 10.2g; Fat: 7.9g; Fiber: 1g; Sugars: 2.3g; Cholesterol: 4mg; Sodium: 318mg

8.9 Fisherman's Stew

Serves: 4 Prep Time: 15 minutes Cook Time: 30 minutes

Ingredients:

- Beef Tallow, 1 tablespoon (15 ml), set to room temperature
- Red Onion, 1 tablespoon (15 ml), chopped
- Garlic, 2 cloves, smashed
- Jalapeno Pepper, 1 piece, seeded and chopped
- Dill Leaves, fresh, ½ bunch, roughly chopped
- Fresh Tomato, 1 ripe, pureed
- Shellfish Stock, 1 cup (237 ml)
- Water, 2 cups (475 ml)
- Halibut, 1 pound (0.45 kg), cut into cubes
- Salt
- Black Pepper, freshly ground
- Cayenne Pepper, 1 teaspoon (5ml)
- Curry Powder, ½ teaspoon (2.5 ml)
- Bay Leaves, 2 pieces

Procedure:

1. Heat the tallow in a large stockpot over a medium high flame. Sauté the onions for 3 minutes in the liquefied tallow. Add the garlic and jalapeno pepper and sauté for 1 minute. Add the fresh dill and tomato puree and cook for 8 more minutes. Pour in the shellfish stock and water. Season with the salt, black pepper, cayenne, and curry powder. Add the bay leaf and the halibut. Cover and allow to cook for 15 minutes or until the halibut is cooked through. Adjust seasonings. Ladle into bowls and serve.

Nutritional Facts: Cal: 271; Carb: 4.8g; Protein: 18.5g; Fat: 19.5g; Fiber: 1g; Sugars: 1.3g; Cholesterol: 74mg; Sodium: 183mg

8.10 Seafood Vegetable Stir-Fry

Serves: 4 Prep Time: 10 minutes Cook Time: 20 minutes

Ingredients:

- Sesame Oil, 1 teaspoon (5ml)
- Scallions, ½ cup, sliced thinly
- Ginger, ½ teaspoon (2.5 ml), grated
- Garlic, ½ teaspoon (2.5 ml), peeled and minced
- Red Curry Paste, 1 teaspoon (5ml)
- Star Anise, 2 pieces
- Smoked Spanish Paprika, 1 teaspoon (5ml)
- Tomatoes, 2 ripe pieces, crushed
- Salt
- Black Pepper, freshly ground
- Snapper Fillet, 1 piece, cut into chunks

Procedure:

1. In a medium skillet, heat the oil over medium heat. Sauté the scallions until tender. Add the garlic and ginger, and sauté until aromatic, for a few seconds. Reduce the heat to a medium-low setting before adding the other ingredients. Allow the fish to simmer for 15 minutes, or until tender. Serve without delay.

Nutritional Facts: Cal: 151; Carb: 5.8g; Protein: 24.4g; Fat: 3g; Fiber: 1.5g; Sugars: 2.8g; Cholesterol: 27mg; Sodium: 144mg

8.11 Salmon Curry

Serves: 4 Prep Time: 10 minutes Cook Time: 20 minutes

Ingredients:

- Coconut Oil, 1 tablespoon (15 ml)
- Leeks, ½ cup, chopped
- Garlic, 1 teaspoon (5ml) minced
- Thai Chili, 1 piece, seeded and minced
- Turmeric, ground, 1 teaspoon (5ml)
- Cilantro Leaves, ¼ cup (32 g), roughly chopped
- Dried Cumin Seed, ½ teaspoon (2.5 ml), ground
- Double Cream, 4 oz. (0.11 kg)
- Black Pepper, freshly ground
- Coconut Milk, 2 oz.,
- Fish Stock, 1 cup (237 ml)
- Water, 1 cup (237 ml)
- Salmon Fillet, ¾ pound, cut into chunks
- Salt

Procedure:

1. Heat the oil in a stockpot over a medium setting and sauté the leeks and garlic for 2 to 3 minutes. Stir frequently. Add the remainder of the ingredients except for the cilantro leaves. Lower the heat to medium low and allow to simmer for 12 minutes or until the fish flakes. Transfer into bowls and serve immediately.

Nutritional Facts: Cal: 246; Carb: 4.9g; Protein: 20.3g; Fat: 16.2g; Fiber: 0.6g; Sugars: 2.1g; Cholesterol: 114mg; Sodium: 219mg

8.12 California Tuna Lettuce Wraps

Serves: 4 Prep Time: 10 minutes Cook Time: 10 minutes plus time to cool.

Ingredients:

- Dry White Wine, ½ cup (118 ml)
- Water, ½ cup (118 ml)
- Peppercorns, ½ teaspoon (2.5 ml)
- Dry Mustard Powder, ½ teaspoon (2.5 ml)
- Ahi Tuna Steak, ½ pound (4 oz.)
- Ham, 6 slices
- Avocado, 1/2 fruit, pitted, peeled and sliced
- Lemon Juice, 1 tablespoon (15 ml)
- Lettuce Leaves, 6 pieces

Procedure:

1. Into a large skillet, add the wine, water, peppercorns and mustard powder. Stir to combine and bring to a boil. Add the tuna and allow to simmer for 4 minutes on each side. Once cooked, remove the tuna and discard the liquid. Slice the tuna into strips and lay on the ham slices. Add the avocado and drizzle with lemon juice. Roll the ham slices up and place on the lettuce leaf. Roll up the lettuce leaf and chill. Serve cold.

Nutritional Facts: Cal: 308; Carb: 4.3g; Protein: 27.8g; Fat: 19.9g; Fiber: 2.5g; Sugars: 0.8g; Cholesterol: 66mg; Sodium: 412mg

8.13 Cod with Mustard Cream Sauce

Serves: 4 Prep Time: 10 minutes Cook Time: 15 minutes

Ingredients:

- Cod Fillets, 4 pieces
- Salt
- Black Pepper, freshly ground
- Parsley Leaves, fresh, 1 tablespoon (15 ml), chopped
- Basil Leaves, 6 pieces, finely chopped
- Yellow Mustard, 1 teaspoon (5ml)
- Coconut Oil, 1 tablespoon (15 ml)
- Spanish Paprika, 1 teaspoon (5ml)
- Bay Leaf, ¼ teaspoon (1.25 ml) crumbled
- Cream Cheese, 3 tablespoons (45 ml)
- Greek Yogurt, ½ cup (118 ml))
- Garlic, 1 clove, peeled and minced
- Lemon Zest, 1 teaspoon (5ml)

Procedure:

1. In a large skillet, heat the oil over medium heat. Season both sides of the cod fillets with pepper, salt and sear for three minutes per side, until the fish is cooked through but not dry.
2. Add the yellow mustard, Spanish paprika, bay leaf, cream cheese, yogurt, garlic, lemon zest and parsley into a pot and stir until well combined over a medium setting. Use to top the cooked cod fillets and garnish with basil leaves. Serve immediately.

Nutritional Facts: Cal: 166; Carb: 2.6g; Protein: 19.8g; Fat: 8.2g; Fiber: 0.3g; Sugars: 1.9g; Cholesterol: 297mg; Sodium: 799mg

8.14 Finnan Haddie Fish Burgers

Serves: 4 Prep Time: 10 minutes Cook Time: 20 minutes

Ingredients:

- Parmesan Cheese, ½ cup (32 g), grated
- Chili Powder, 1 teaspoon (5ml)
- Parsley Leaves, dried, 1 teaspoon (5ml)
- Egg, 1 whole
- Scallions, ¼ cup (32 g), chopped
- Garlic, 1 teaspoon (5ml) peeled and minced
- Sunflower Oil, 2 tablespoons (30 ml)
- Salt
- Smoked Haddock, 8 oz. (0.23 kg),
- Black Pepper, freshly ground
- Lemon Wedges, 4 pieces

Procedure:

1. In a skillet, heat one tablespoon of the oil over a medium-high burner. Cook the haddock for six minutes, or until it reaches the desired doneness. Remove the skin and bones from the meat, then flake it. In a bowl, combine the haddock meat with the remaining ingredients and form four patties.
2. Six minutes later, heat the remaining tablespoon of oil and cook the fish patties until well done. Serve with a lemon wedge garnish.

Nutritional Facts: Cal: 174; Carb: 1.5g; Protein: 15.4g; Fat: 11.4g; Fiber: 0.2g; Sugars: 0.3g; Cholesterol: 185mg; Sodium: 1531mg

9 SIDES

9.1 Cauliflower Risotto

Serves: 6 Prep Time: 10 minutes Cook Time: 20 minutes

Ingredients:

- Butter, ¼ cup (32 g)
- Shallots, 2 pieces, peeled and minced
- Black Pepper, freshly ground
- Garlic, 3 cloves, peeled and minced
- Salt
- Parmesan Cheese, ½ cup (32 g), grated
- Cauliflower Rice, 6 cups (1419.5 g)
- Baby Portobello Mushrooms, 1 ½ cups (350 ml), sliced thinly
- Half and Half, ¾ cup (175 ml)
- Nutmeg, ¼ teaspoon (1.25 ml) ground

Procedure:

1. Melt the butter over a medium heat setting in a skillet. The shallots and garlic should be cooked for 5 minutes, until softened. Cook the riced cauliflower and mushrooms for 6 minutes. Stir in the remaining ingredients to mix them. Continue cooking for six minutes, or until the cauliflower is tender. Allow to cool before serving, or refrigerate in six-portion airtight containers for up to one week.

Nutritional Facts: Cal: 179; Carb: 6g; Protein: 6g; Fat: 13g; Fiber: 3g; Sugars: 4g; Cholesterol: 36mg; Sodium: 586mg

9.2 Haricot Verts Casserole

Serves: 6 Prep Time: 10 minutes Cook Time: 30 minutes

Ingredients:

- Green Beans, fresh, 1 pound (0.45 kg), trimmed and halved
- Butter, 2 tablespoons (30 ml)
- Shallot, 1 large, peeled and minced
- Garlic, 3 cloves, minced
- Chicken Stock, ½ cup (32 g)
- Heavy Cream, ½ cup (118 ml)
- Parmesan Cheese, ½ cup (32 g), grated
- Pork Rinds, ½ cup (32 g), crushed

Procedure:

1. Heat up an oven to 400°F. Prepare a 9x13-inch baking dish by greasing it with oil. Set aside.
2. Fill a big pot with salt-seasoned water. Blanch the beans for 5 minutes to soften them somewhat while maintaining their crispness. Remove the object from the water and set it aside.
3. In a large skillet, melt the butter over medium heat and sauté the shallots and garlic for 5 minutes, or until tender. Bring the chicken broth and cream to a boil over high heat. Reduce the heat to low and simmer for about 5 minutes to thicken the sauce. Then, add the blanched green beans and whisk in the parmesan cheese until it has melted.
4. Transfer the mixture to the prepared baking dish and top with the pork rind crumbs. Bake in the heated oven for 15 minutes or until the sauce is bubbly and rinds become brown. Allow to cool before serving or storing in an airtight container in the refrigerator for up to one week.

Nutritional Facts: Cal: 169; Carb: 5g; Protein: 3.5g; Fat: 12g; Fiber: 2g; Sugars: 3g; Cholesterol: 51mg; Sodium: 94mg

9.3 Hellenic Spinach

Serves: 6 Prep Time: 10 minutes Cook Time: 15 minutes

Ingredients:

- Shallots, 3 large, peeled and minced
- Lemon Juice, 2 tablespoons (30 ml)
- Garlic, 4 cloves, peeled and minced
- Butter, 2 tablespoons (30 ml)
- Oregano Leaves, dried, 1 teaspoon (5ml)
- Frozen Spinach, 2 (10 oz.) packages, thawed, drained and squeezed
- Lemon Zest, 1 teaspoon (5ml)
- Feta Cheese, ½ cup (32 g), crumbled

Procedure:

1. On a medium heat setting, melt the butter in a skillet and sauté the shallots and garlic for three minutes, until softened. Add the lemon juice, lemon zest, oregano, spinach, and simmer for an additional three minutes. Sprinkle feta over the spinach and toss to mix. Allow to cool before serving. Additionally, you may store in six sealed containers in the refrigerator for up to one week.

Nutritional Facts: Cal: 98; Carb: 2g; Protein: 5g; Fat: 12g; Fiber: 3g; Sugars: 1g; Cholesterol: 21mg; Sodium: 185mg

9.4 Lemon Pepper Haricot Verts

Serves: 6 Prep Time: 10 minutes Cook Time: 15 minutes

Ingredients:

- Green Beans, 1 pound (0.45 kg), trimmed
- Butter, 2 tablespoons (30 ml)
- Lemon Juice, 1 tablespoon (15 ml)
- Lemon Pepper, 1 teaspoon (5ml)
- Salt
- Black Pepper, freshly ground

Procedure:

1. Steam the green beans for 8 minutes on high in a steamer basket placed over a saucepan of boiling water, until cooked but still slightly crisp. Drain and reserve.
2. In a medium skillet, melt the butter and add the green beans. Add the lemon juice and toss the beans to coat with it. Season with salt, lemon pepper, and black pepper. Toss and allow to cool. Serve immediately or refrigerate in sealed containers for up to one week.

Nutritional Facts: Cal: 57; Carb: 3g; Protein: 1.5g; Fat: 4g; Fiber: 2g; Sugars: 2g; Cholesterol: 10mg; Sodium: 102mg

9.5 Cauliflower Spanakorizo

Serves: 6 Prep Time: 10 minutes Cook Time: 15 minutes

Ingredients:

- Butter, 2 tablespoons (30 ml)
- Onion, 1 yellow, large, peeled and diced
- Garlic, 2 cloves, peeled and minced
- Frozen Spinach, 1 (10 oz.) package, thawed, drained and squeezed
- Cauliflower Rice, 1 (12 oz.) package, thawed
- Salt
- Black Pepper, freshly ground
- Dill Leaves, dried, ½ teaspoon (2.5 ml)
- Feta Cheese, ½ cup (32 g), crumbled

Procedure:

1. In a skillet, melt the butter over medium heat and sauté the garlic and onion for three minutes, until softened. Add the spinach and heat for approximately 2 minutes. Add the remaining ingredients, excluding the feta cheese, and boil the cauliflower for about 7 minutes, or until soft. Remove from heat and top with crumbled feta.
2. Let cool before serving or store in airtight containers for up to a week in the fridge.

Nutritional Facts: Cal: 104; Carb: 5g; Protein: 5g; Fat: 6g; Fiber: 3g; Sugars: 3g; Cholesterol: 21mg; Sodium: 557mg

9.6 Roasted Cauliflower

Serves: 6 Prep Time: 10 minutes Cook Time: 20 minutes

Ingredients:

- Garlic, 2 tablespoons (30 ml), minced
- Olive Oil, 3 tablespoons (45 ml)
- Cauliflower, 1 large head, broken into florets
- Salt
- Black Pepper, freshly ground
- Onion Powder, ¾ teaspoon
- Parsley Leaves, fresh, 1 tablespoon (15 ml), chopped
- Parmesan Cheese, ¼ cup (32 g), grated

Procedure:

1. Heat up an oven to 450 degrees Fahrenheit. Spray a 9 x 13" baking tray with oil and set aside.
2. In a large bowl, mix together the olive oil and garlic. Toss in the cauliflower florets to coat. Add parsley, onion powder, black pepper, salt, and mix once more to coat. Transfer the cauliflower to the prepared baking dish and bake, covered, for 15 minutes, or until soft. Allow the Parmesan to broil for three minutes, until the cheese is golden brown.
3. Let cool and serve or transfer into 6 airtight containers and store in the ref for up to a week.

Nutritional Facts: Cal: 107; Carb: 4g; Protein: 3g; Fat: 8g; Fiber: 2g; Sugars: 2g; Cholesterol: 16mg; Sodium: 493mg

9.7 Sautéed Mixed Peppers

Serves: 6 Prep Time: 10 minutes Cook Time: 10 minutes

Ingredients:

- Butter, 3 tablespoons (45 ml)
- Red Capsicum, medium, 1 piece, seeded and julienned
- Yellow Capsicum, medium, 1 piece, seeded and julienned
- Orange Capsicum, medium ,1 piece, seeded and julienned
- Red Onions, 2 medium pieces, thinly sliced
- Salt
- Black Pepper, freshly ground
- Italian Herb Mix

Procedure:

1. In a skillet, melt the butter over medium heat and sauté the peppers and onions for eight minutes, or until tender. Toss with salt, pepper, and Italian Herb Mix to coat. Remove from heat and allow to cool before serving or refrigerate for up to one week in airtight containers.

Nutritional Facts: Cal: 79; Carb: 4g; Protein: 1g; Fat: 6g; Fiber: 2g; Sugars: 3g; Cholesterol: 15mg; Sodium: 101mg

9.8 Creamed Cucumber

Serves: 6 Prep Time: 10 minutes Cook Time: 0 minutes

Ingredients:

- Coconut Oil Mayonnaise, 1 ½ cups (350 ml)
- Heavy Cream, ¼ cup (32 g)
- Granulated Erythritol, 1 teaspoon (5ml)
- White Vinegar, ¾ teaspoon
- Dill Leaves, dried, ½ teaspoon (2.5 ml)
- Salt
- Black Pepper, freshly ground
- Cucumbers, 2 large, sliced thinly

Procedure:

1. In a large bowl, thoroughly combine all of the ingredients, excluding the cucumbers, except for the cucumbers. Toss the cucumbers with the dressing to evenly coat them. Serve immediately or refrigerate for up to one week in sealed containers.

Nutritional Facts: Cal: 442; Carb: 3.5g; Protein: 1g; Fat: 47g; Fiber: 0.5g; Sugars: 2g; Cholesterol: 34mg; Sodium: 512mg

9.9 Mediterranean Zucchini

Serves: 6 Prep Time: 10 minutes Cook Time: 10 minutes

Ingredients:

- Butter, ¼ cup (32 g)
- Zucchini, 4 medium pieces, sliced crosswise
- Dill Leaves, dried, 2 teaspoons (10 ml)
- Lemon Juice, 1 tablespoon (15 ml)
- Salt
- Black Pepper, freshly ground

Procedure:

1. In a medium skillet heated over medium heat, sauté the zucchini until tender but still somewhat crunchy, about 4 minutes. Add the other ingredients and toss the zucchini to coat. Continue cooking for two minutes, then remove from heat. Serve immediately or refrigerate in sealed containers for up to one week.

Nutritional Facts: Cal: 91; Carb: 2.5g; Protein: 2g; Fat: 8g; Fiber: 1.5g; Sugars: 3g; Cholesterol: 20mg; Sodium: 206mg

9.10 Creamed Onions

Serves: 6 Prep Time: 10 minutes Cook Time: 25 minutes

Ingredients:

- Butter, 4 tablespoons
- Onions, 2 large yellow, peeled and sliced
- Garlic, 2 cloves, peeled and minced
- Half and Half, 1 cup (237 ml)
- Salt
- Black Pepper, freshly ground
- Parmesan Cheese, 2/3 cup, grated
- Mozzarella Cheese, ¼ cup (32 g), grated

Procedure:

1. Heat up an oven to 425 degrees Fahrenheit and prepare a 9 x 9" baking dish.
2. In a medium skillet, melt the butter over medium heat and sauté the onions and garlic until tender, about 5 minutes. Transfer to the baking dish you have prepared.
3. Whisk the half-and-half, salt, and pepper in a small bowl until foamy, then pour over the onions that have been sautéed. Allow the cheeses to bubble for 15 minutes in the oven after being sprinkled on top. Remove from the oven and allow to cool before to serving. This can be refrigerated for up to a week in sealed containers.

Nutritional Facts: Cal: 205; Carb: 6g; Protein: 7g; Fat: 16g; Fiber: 1g; Sugars: 4g; Cholesterol: 44mg; Sodium: 417mg

10 POULTRY

10.1 Artichoke Chicken Wrapped in Bacon

Serves: 4 Prep Time: 15 minutes Cook Time: 45 minutes

Ingredients:

- Chicken Thighs, deboned and skinned, 4 pieces
- Artichoke Hearts, ¾ cup (175 ml), canned
- Avocado Oil, 2 tablespoons (30 ml)
- Basil Leaves
- Garlic, 2 cloves
- Salt
- Black Pepper, freshly ground
- Bacon, 12 strips
- Arugula, 8 cups, divided into 4 portions

Procedure:

1. Heat up the oven to 400 degrees Fahrenheit. Prepare a baking sheet with a rim and line either with greaseproof parchment or a silpad. Set aside.
2. On another sheet of parchment, lay out the deboned and skinned chicken thighs and flatten them with a meat mallet or rolling pin until ¼ inch thick, Set aside.
3. Into the jar of a food processor or blender, add all of the ingredients except for the bacon and arugula. Pulse until chopped, but do not puree. Spread a quarter of this mixture onto the flattened chicken thighs starting from the short end of the thigh. Leave about an inch from the edge of the thigh. Roll the thigh and wrap with three bacon strips. Set, seam side down on the prepared baking tray. Repeat with the other thighs.
4. Bake in the heated oven for 45 minutes or until the internal temperature of the chicken registers 165 degrees Fahrenheit and the bacon is crisp. Serve

1 thigh with 2 cups (64 g)of Arugula. Dress the arugula with the chicken drippings and toss lightly.

Nutritional Facts: Cal: 666; Carb: 4.3g; Protein: 53.1g; Fat: 47.4g; Fiber: 2.5g; Sugars: 1.2g; Cholesterol: 189mg; Sodium: 2223mg

10.2 Autumnal Chicken Thighs

Serves: 6 Prep Time: 15 minutes Cook Time: 30 minutes

Ingredients:

- Black Pepper, freshly ground
- Chicken Thighs, deboned and skinned, 6 small pieces or 3 large pieces
- Coconut Oil, ¼ cup (32 g)
- Onion Powder, ½ teaspoon (2.5 ml)
- Salt
- Butternut Squash, 1 medium piece, peeled and seeded
- Ghee, 2 tablespoons (30 ml)
- Garlic Powder, 1 teaspoon (5ml)
- Milk, Non-dairy, 1/3 cup (75 ml)
- Chicken Stock, 1 ½ cups (350 ml)

Procedure:

1. Heat up an oven to 400 degrees Fahrenheit. Prepare a rimmed baking sheet and line with a silicone pad or greaseproof parchment and set aside. If using large chicken thighs, halve them to make 6 servings. Arrange the chicken on the prepared baking sheet and drizzle with the coconut oil. Season with the garlic powder, onion powder, salt and pepper and rub all over the chicken to coat evenly. Bake for 25 to 30 minutes or until the internal temperature of the chicken registers 165 degrees Fahrenheit. Slice into ½ inch pieces.
2. Cut the prepared squash into cubes and use about 3 cups (360 g) of the cubed squash. Reserve the rest for another use. Heat the ghee in a large pan over a

medium setting and add the squash. Season with salt and pepper. Cover with a lid and cook for 10 to 15 minutes until the squash is slightly browned. Pour the milk and stock and cover. Let cook for another 15 minutes or until the squash has softened. Once it is soft enough to mash, use a potato masher and mash the squash in the pan. Portion into 6 plates and serve with the chicken.

Nutritional Facts: Cal: 331; Carb: 8.3g; Protein: 16.2g; Fat: 26.5g; Fiber: 1.6g; Sugars: 1.8g; Cholesterol: 91mg; Sodium: 613mg

10.3 Creamy Mushroom Chicken

Serves: 4 Prep Time: 10 minutes Cook Time: 45 minutes

Ingredients:

- Coconut Oil, 3 tablespoons (45 ml)
- Chestnut Mushrooms, 7 oz., brushed and chopped
- Garlic, 4 cloves, peeled and minced
- Parsley Leaves, dried, 3 teaspoons divided into 1 ½ teaspoons (5.9 g)
- Salt
- Black Pepper, freshly ground
- Chicken Breasts, deboned, skin-on, 1 pound (0.45 kg)
- Onion Powder, 1 teaspoon (5ml)
- Garlic Powder, 1 teaspoon (5ml)
- Milk, ½ cup (118 ml), non-dairy or regular
- Spinach Leaves, 4 cups, rinsed

Procedure:

1. Preheat the oven to 400°F. Prepare a rimmed baking sheet by lining it with a silicone pad or non-stick parchment paper and setting it aside.
2. In a large skillet, heat the oil over medium heat and sauté the garlic and mushrooms. Season with half of the parsley, salt, and pepper, and simmer the mushrooms for 10 minutes while turning to evenly distribute the flavours.
3. Create a pocket in each chicken breast with a knife. Do not cut completely through. Place the chicken breasts on the prepared baking sheet and divide the mushroom mixture among each pocket. Fold over the chicken breasts to protect the mushroom mixture. Season the chicken with the onion and garlic powders, the parsley and salt. Pour milk onto the chicken breasts and bake for 32 minutes or until the internal temperature of the chicken registers 165 degrees Fahrenheit.
4. Portion the spinach onto 4 plates and serve with a portion of chicken breasts. Serve with the drippings.

Nutritional Facts: Cal: 388; Carb: 4.3g; Protein: 38.2g; Fat: 24.3g; Fiber: 2.3g; Sugars: 1.6g; Cholesterol: 96mg; Sodium: 492mg

10.4 Chicken Pesto Pasta

Serves: 4 Prep Time: 10 minutes Cook Time: 20 minutes

Ingredients:

- Avocado Oil, ¼ cup (32 g)
- Chicken Breasts, deboned and skinned, 1 pound (0.45 kg), thinly sliced
- Onion, 1 small white, peeled and thinly sliced
- Sun-Dried Tomatoes, ½ cup (32 g), drained and chopped
- Oregano Leaves, dried, ¾ teaspoon
- Thyme Leaves, dried, ½ teaspoon (2.5 ml)
- Red Pepper Flakes, 1/8 teaspoon (0.6g)
- Garlic, 2 cloves
- Piñoli, ¼ cup (32 g)
- Nutritional Yeast, ¼ cup (32 g)
- Chicken Stock, ½ cup (118 ml)
- Coconut Milk, ½ cup (118 ml)
- Salt
- Black Pepper, freshly ground
- Basil Leaves, ½ oz.,
- Zucchinis, 2 medium pieces, spiralized

Procedure:

1. Heat oil in a big skillet over a medium setting. Toss the chicken, onions, tomatoes, oregano, thyme, and red pepper flakes to evenly coat. Sauté for 5 minutes until fragrant.
2. In a food processor, combine the garlic, Piñoli, yeast, stock, coconut milk, salt, and pepper for 30 seconds. Add basil and process. Currently, the sauce should not be green. Pour the sauce into the pan containing the chicken and toss to coat the chicken with the sauce. Reduce the heat and cover the pan with a lid. Allow to cook for 15 minutes, stirring regularly to ensure the chicken is cooked through.
3. Spiralize some zucchini and serve it alongside the chicken.

Nutritional Facts: Cal: 455; Carb: 11.4.g; Protein: 32.2g; Fat: 29.3g; Fiber: 4.4g; Sugars: 3.3g; Cholesterol: 74mg; Sodium: 437mg

10.5 Feta Turkey Patties

Serves: 6 Prep Time: 10 minutes Cook Time: 10 minutes

Ingredients:

- Turkey Mince, 1 ½ pounds
- Feta Cheese, crumbled, 1 ½ cups (350 ml)
- Garlic, 1 clove, peeled and minced
- Chicken Stock, ¼ cup (32 g)
- Kalamata Olives, pitted and minced, ½ cup (43 g)
- Greek Seasoning, 2 teaspoons (10 ml)
- Black Pepper, freshly ground
- Coconut Oil, 2 tablespoons (30 ml)

Procedure:

1. Besides the oil, combine the remaining ingredients in a bowl. Mix thoroughly and form six patties. In a large skillet, heat the oil on medium and add the patties. Cook for five minutes per side, or until done. Remove from heat and allow to cool slightly before to serving, or refrigerate in airtight containers for up to one week.

Nutritional Facts: Cal: 318; Carb: 5.g; Protein: 27g; Fat: 21g; Fiber: 0g; Sugars: 1g; Cholesterol: 123mg; Sodium: 412mg

10.6 Cheesy Chicken Casserole

Serves: 6 Prep Time: 20 minutes Cook Time: 1 hour

Ingredients:

- Mozzarella Cheese, shredded, 1 cup (237 ml)
- Cheddar Cheese, grated, 1 cup (237 ml)
- Butter, 3 tablespoons (45 ml)
- Yellow Onion, peeled and diced, 1 small piece
- Lemon Juice, 1 teaspoon (5ml)
- Chicken Stock, 1 cup (237 ml)
- Black Pepper, freshly ground
- Garlic, minced, 2 teaspoons (10 ml)
- Garlic Salt, ½ teaspoon (2.5 ml)
- Parsley Leaves, dried, ¼ teaspoon (1.25 ml)
- Salt
- Cauliflower Rice, 2 cups (400 g)
- Heavy Cream, 1 cup (237 ml)
- Mayonnaise, ½ cup (118 ml)
- Chicken Breasts, deboned and skinned, cooked and shredded, 1 ½ pounds
- Broccoli Florets, steamed and chopped, 4 cups

Procedure:

1. Heat up an oven to 350 degrees Fahrenheit. Prepare a 9"x13" baking dish and set aside.
2. In a large saucepan, melt the butter over medium heat and sauté the onions and garlic until tender, about 6 minutes. Season with garlic salt, parsley, pepper, and salt. Stir in the cauliflower rice. Add the chicken stock and cook for approximately 10 minutes, or until the cauliflower has absorbed the fluid.
3. Stir in the heavy cream and the lemon juice. Lower the heat to low and let simmer. Remove from the flame and stir the mayonnaise in.
4. Spread the cooked chicken in a single layer in the prepared baking dish and pour the cauliflower rice mixture on top. Stir to combine and spread with a spatula. Top with the broccoli and pour the remainder of the cauliflower mixture over the broccoli. Sprinkle with the cheese and let bake in the heated oven for 30 minutes, covered. Remove the cover and broil for 10 minutes until the cheese are bubbly.
5. Let cool and cut into 6 portions and serve. You may store in airtight containers for up to a week in the refrigerator.

Nutritional Facts: Cal: 642; Carb: 6.5g; Protein: 38g; Fat: 50g; Fiber: 2.5g; Sugars: 3.5g; Cholesterol: 223mg; Sodium: 816mg

10.7 Chicken Cordon with a Twist

Serves: 6 Prep Time: 10 minutes Cook Time: 35 minutes

Ingredients:

- Bacon, sugar-free, 1 pound (0.45 kg)
- Yellow Onion, peeled and diced, 1 large piece
- Granulated Erythritol, ¼ cup (32 g)
- Coconut Aminos, 2 teaspoons (10 ml)
- Salt
- Lemon Pepper, ½ teaspoon (2.5 ml)
- Chicken Breasts, deboned and skinned, 6 (4 oz.) pieces
- Avocado Oil, 2 tablespoons (30 ml)
- Monterey Jack Cheese, grated, 1 cup (237 ml)

Procedure:

1. Heat up an oven to 350 degrees Fahrenheit. Heat a large oven-proof skillet and cook the bacon over a medium setting. Transfer the cooked bacon on a paper towel-lined plate to drain. Reserve the rendered bacon fat in the pan.
2. Heat the reserved bacon fat in the pan over a medium setting and sauté the onions, and season with the erythritol and coconut aminos. Caramelize the onions in the pan for about 10 minutes. Chop the bacon and stir into the caramelized onions. Remove from the flame.
3. The chicken breasts are seasoned with salt and lemon pepper, and avocado oil is added to a fresh skillet heated to medium temperature. Cook the chicken breasts for 7 minutes on one side and 8 minutes on the other until cooked fully. The chicken breasts are topped with an equal amount of the onion and bacon mixture and cheese. Cover the skillet and allow the cheese to melt for approximately 3 minutes.
4. Remove from pan and allow to cool before you serve, or store in an airtight container for up to week in the fridge.

Nutritional Facts: Cal: 585; Carb: 10.5g; Protein: 40g; Fat: 44g; Fiber: 0.5g; Sugars: 1.5g; Cholesterol: 104mg; Sodium: 748mg

10.8 Turkey Bacon Meatloaf

Serves: 6 Prep Time: 10 minutes Cook Time: 1 hour

Ingredients:

- Bacon, sugar-free, cooked and crumbled, 6 slices
- Turkey Mince, 1 ½ pounds
- Cheddar Cheese, grated, 1 cup (237 ml)
- Egg, 1 large piece
- Yellow Onion, peeled and diced, 1 small
- Coconut Aminos, 1 tablespoon (15 ml)
- Granulated Garlic, 2 teaspoons (10 ml)
- Dry Mustard, 1 teaspoon (5ml)
- Black Pepper, freshly ground
- Ketchup, sugar-free, ½ cup (43g) divided into ¼ cup (32 g) portions

Procedure:

1. Heat up an oven to 350 degrees Fahrenheit and prepare a 9"x 5" loaf pan.
2. In a large bowl, combine all of the ingredients, excluding the 1/4 cup (32 g) of ketchup, using your hands. Transfer the meat to the loaf pan and brush with the remaining 1/4 cup (32 g) ketchup. Bake for one hour or until an internal temperature of 165 degrees Fahrenheit is reached. Take from oven and allow to cool. Serve immediately or refrigerate for up to one week in an airtight container.

Nutritional Facts: Cal: 415; Carb: 8.5g; Protein: 32g; Fat: 27g; Fiber: 0.5g; Sugars: 5g; Cholesterol: 192mg; Sodium: 619mg

10.9 Mozzarella in Meatballs

Serves: 6 Prep Time: 10 minutes Cook Time: 30 minutes

Ingredients:

- Turkey Mince 1 ½ pounds
- Yellow Onion, minced, ½ cup (43 g)
- Garlic, minced, 2 cloves
- Egg, 1 large
- Almond Meal, ½ cup (43 g)
- Italian Herb Mix, ½ teaspoon (2.5 ml)
- Parmesan Cheese, grated, ¼ cup (32 g)
- Parsley Leaves, fresh, ¼ cup (32 g), chopped
- Basil Leaves, dried, 1 teaspoon (5ml)
- Chicken Stock, 2 tablespoons (30 ml)
- Salt
- Black Pepper, freshly ground
- Mozzarella Cheese, ½ pound, cut into 18 cubes

Procedure:

1. Heat up an oven to 375 degrees Fahrenheit and line a baking sheet with greaseproof parchment and set aside.
2. Add all of the ingredients except for the mozzarella into a large bowl and mix with your hands until well combined. Portion into 18 pieces and insert a mozzarella cube into the middle of each. Reroll into a ball and set on the prepared tray. Bake for 30 minutes until meatballs are cooked through and browned. Remove from oven and let cool before serving. Store in an airtight container if need be, for up to a week in the fridge.

Nutritional Facts: Cal: 336; Carb: 9.5g; Protein: 32g; Fat: 17g; Fiber: 0.5g; Sugars: 1g; Cholesterol: 157mg; Sodium: 894mg

10.10 Buffalo Blue Cheese Burgers

Serves: 6 Prep Time: 10 minutes plus 1 hour to chill Cook Time: 20 minutes

Ingredients:

- Chicken Mince, 1 ½ pounds
- Almond Meal, 1 ½ cups (350 ml)
- Blue Cheese, crumbled, ¾ cup (175 ml)
- Egg, 1 large
- Minced Onion, dried, 2 tablespoons (30 ml)
- Hot Sauce, ½ cup (118 ml)

Procedure:

1. Combine all of the ingredients in a large bowl and mix with your hands until fully incorporated. Chill for an hour.
2. Heat up an oven to 350°F. Line a baking sheet with non-stick parchment paper. Form the mixture into six patties and place them on the baking sheet. Bake for 20 minutes, flipping once, or until the internal temperature reaches 165°F.
3. Let cool and serve, or store in an airtight container for up to a week in the fridge.

Nutritional Facts: Cal: 436; Carb: 5g; Protein: 26g; Fat: 24g; Fiber: 1g; Sugars: 0.5g; Cholesterol: 233mg; Sodium: 296mg

10.11 Thai Chicken Satay and Rice

Serves: 6 Prep Time: 10 minutes Cook Time: 20 minutes

Ingredients:

- Coconut Aminos, 6 tablespoons (90 ml)
- Creamy Peanut Butter, sugar-free, 4 tablespoons
- White Wine Vinegar, 4 teaspoons
- Cayenne Pepper, ¼ teaspoon (1.25 ml)
- Peanut Oil, 3 tablespoons (45 ml)
- Chicken Breasts, deboned and skinned, cut into strips, 1 ½ pounds
- Garlic, 2 tablespoons (30 ml), minced
- Ginger Root, minced, 1 tablespoon (15 ml)
- Scallions, chopped, ½ cup (43 g)
- Broccoli Florets, 2 ½ cups
- Peanuts, 1/3 cup (75 ml), roasted
- Cauliflower Rice, 2 cups (400 g)
- Cilantro Leaves, fresh, ½ cup (43 g)

Procedure:

1. In a small bowl, combine the coconut aminos, peanut butter, white wine vinegar and cayenne pepper and mix. Set aside.
2. In a wok heated over high heat, sauté the chicken, garlic, and ginger for 5 minutes, or until the chicken begins to brown.
3. Add the scallions, broccoli florets, peanuts, and coconut aminos combination and reduce the heat to medium. Cook for five minutes while stirring continuously. Add cauliflower rice to the mixture and toss to distribute evenly. Cook for four minutes, or until the cauliflower rice is done and the broccoli is soft. The chicken should also be thoroughly cooked. Add the cilantro and turn off the heat.
4. Let cool and serve, or store in 6 airtight containers for up to a week in the refrigerator.

Nutritional Facts: Cal: 342; Carb: 7g; Protein: 31g; Fat: 20g; Fiber: 3g; Sugars: 3g; Cholesterol: 191mg; Sodium: 260mg

10.12 Mediterranean Chicken Bake

Serves: 6 Prep Time: 10 minutes Cook Time: 50 minutes

Ingredients:

- Butter, ½ cup (118 ml)
- Coconut Aminos, 3 tablespoons (45 ml)
- Garlic, 3 tablespoons (45 ml), minced
- Black Pepper, freshly ground
- Rosemary Leaves, 1 tablespoon (15 ml)
- Chicken Thighs, with skin, deboned, 6 4 oz. (0.11 kg) pieces

Procedure:

1. Heat up an oven to 375 degrees Fahrenheit and prepare a medium sized baking dish.
2. In a small sauce pan, combine all of the ingredients except for the chicken and allow to liquefy together over a medium setting. Let cook for 3 minutes and stir occasionally.
3. Place the chicken in the baking dish that has been prepared. Spread the melted butter on the chicken. Bake for 45 minutes, or until the chicken is thoroughly done. Halfway through the Cooking time, flip the food. Cool before serving. Additionally, chicken thighs may be stored in containers for up to one week.

Nutritional Facts: Cal: 279; Carb: 0.5g; Protein: 22g; Fat: 20g; Fiber: 0.5g; Sugars: 0g; Cholesterol: 421mg; Sodium: 314mg

10.13 Roasted Provencal Turkey

Serves: 6 Prep Time: 10 minutes Cook Time: 2 hours and 30 minutes

Ingredients:

- Olive Oil, ½ cup (118 ml)
- Garlic, minced, 2 tablespoons (30 ml)
- Rosemary Leaves, fresh, chopped 2 tablespoons (30 ml)
- Rosemary Sprigs, 2 pieces
- Basil Leaves, fresh, 2 tablespoons (30 ml)
- Italian Herb Mix, dried, 1 tablespoon (15 ml)
- Salt
- Black Pepper, freshly ground
- Whole Turkey, 1 6 pound bird
- Onion, 1 yellow, peeled and quartered
- Chicken Stock, 2 cups (475 ml)

Procedure:

1. Heat up an oven to 350 degrees Fahrenheit and prepare a large roasting pan.
2. To make the rub, combine the pepper, salt, Italian Herb mix, basil, rosemary leaves, garlic, and olive oil in a small bowl, and then rub it all over the turkey with your hands. Rub it into every nook and cranny. Stuff the interior of the turkey with the quartered onions and rosemary sprigs.
3. Set the turkey in the roasting pan and pour the chicken broth into the pan. Roast for 2 and a half hours or until the internal temperature of the turkey reads 165 degrees Fahrenheit in the thickest part. Let cool and slice the turkey before you serve. You can also store this for up to a week in airtight containers.

Nutritional Facts: Cal: 185; Carb: 3.5g; Protein: 6.3g; Fat: 18g; Fiber: 0.5g; Sugars: 1g; Cholesterol: 11mg; Sodium: 413mg

10.14 Bacon Basted Chicken Thighs

Serves: 6 Prep Time: 10 minutes Cook Time: 40 minutes

Ingredients:

- Salt
- Black Pepper, freshly ground
- Chicken Thighs, deboned and skinned, 1 ½ pounds
- Bacon, sugar-free, 12 slices
- Onion, 1 medium yellow, peeled and chopped

Procedure:

1. Prepare an oven to 400° F and a 9-by-13-inch baking dish. The chicken thighs are seasoned with salt and pepper. Wrap the chicken thighs in bacon and secure with skewers. Transfer the meat to the prepared baking dish and top with the onions.
2. Bake the chicken for 40 minutes, flipping it after 20 minutes. Turn the oven to broil and continue cooking for three minutes, or until the bacon is crisp and the chicken is fully cooked. Remove from heat and allow to gently cool before serving. You may also make this a week in advance and store it in the refrigerator.

Nutritional Facts: Cal: 376; Carb: 2g; Protein: 29g; Fat: 26g; Fiber: 0.5g; Sugars: 1g; Cholesterol: 232mg; Sodium: 803mg

11 APPETIZERS

11.1 Crisp Yam Bean Fries

Serves: 4 Prep Time: 5 minutes Cook Time: 40 minutes

Ingredients:

- Jicama, cut into French-fry sized pieces, 1 medium piece, peeled
- Avocado Oil, 2 tablespoons (30 ml)
- Spanish Paprika, ½ teaspoon (2.5 ml)
- Salt
- Parsley Leaves, finely chopped, 1 tablespoon (15 ml)
- Mayonnaise or Ketchup, ½ cup (118 ml) for a dip

Procedure:

1. Preheat the oven to 400°F and prepare a rimmed baking sheet with non-stick parchment paper or a silicone pad. Spread the jicama slices on this baking sheet and drizzle with oil and paprika. Hand-mix the ingredients and bake the fries for forty minutes. Turn after 20 minutes.
2. Remove the fries from the oven and season with the salt and parsley leaves. Toss to coat evenly. Serve with the mayonnaise or ketchup.

Nutritional Facts: Cal: 276; Carb: 6.5g; Protein: 1.2g; Fat: 23.7g; Fiber: 8.2g; Sugars: 3g; Cholesterol: 10mg; Sodium: 245mg

11.2 Salad Dippers

Serves: 4 Prep Time: 5 minutes Cook Time: 0 minutes

Ingredients:

- Iceberg Lettuce, cut into wedges 1 medium head
- Ranch Dressing, ½ cup (118 ml)

Procedure:

1. Slice the lettuce into wedges until you have 16 pieces. Serve with the ranch dressing on the side.

Nutritional Facts: Cal: 132; Carb: 4.6g; Protein: 0.8g; Fat: 12.3g; Fiber: 0.9g; Sugars: 1.4g; Cholesterol: 0mg; Sodium: 111mg

11.3 Avocado Bacon Fries

Serves: 4 Prep Time: 10 minutes Cook Time: 18 minutes

Ingredients:

- Hass Avocados, pitted, peeled and sliced, 2 medium pieces
- Bacon, 16 strips

Procedure:

1. Slice each avocado into 8 pieces for a total of 16 pieces from 2 avocados. Wrap each in two strips of bacon and set each finished piece in a large skillet. Heat the pan over a medium flame and cover with a lid to reduce splatters. Fry for 6 minutes each side in the rendered bacon fat for a total of 18 minutes until the bacon is crisp. Remove from heat and serve immediately.

Nutritional Facts: Cal: 723; Carb: 6.4g; Protein: 43.2g; Fat: 58.3g; Fiber: 3.7g; Sugars: 0.3g; Cholesterol: 125mg; Sodium: 2631mg

11.4 Not-Chicken Nuggets

Serves: 4 Prep Time: 10 minutes Cook Time: 50 minutes

- Salt

Ingredients:

- Chestnut Mushrooms, 2 dozen pieces, stems removed.
- Eggs, 2 large pieces
- Spanish Paprika, 1 teaspoon (5ml)
- Almond Meal, ½ cup (43 g)
- Garlic Powder, 1 teaspoon (5ml)
- Avocado Oil, 2 tablespoons (30 ml)
- Honey Mustard Dressing, ½ cup (118 ml) for dip

Procedure:

1. Heat up an oven to 350 degrees Fahrenheit. Line a rimmed baking tray with a silpad or greaseproof parchment. Set aside.
2. The stems of the mushrooms should be removed or clipped. Prepare your station for breading: In a bowl, whisk two eggs and set aside. In a separate bowl, thoroughly combine the salt, Spanish paprika, garlic powder and almond meal.
3. Dip the mushrooms into the egg mixture, then dredge in the almond meal mixture. Coat on all sides with the help of a fork or tweezers and set on the prepared baking tray. Repeat with the rest of the mushrooms. Drizzle them with oil and bake in the heated oven for 50 minutes or until browned. Serve with the honey mustard dressing to dip.

Nutritional Facts: Cal: 332; Carb: 7.3g; Protein: 8g; Fat: 29.3g; Fiber: 2g; Sugars: 4.5g; Cholesterol: 93mg; Sodium: 398mg

11.5 Cucumber and Salmon Canapés

Serves: 2 Prep Time: 5 minutes Cook Time: 0 minutes

Ingredients:

- English Cucumber, 1 piece, sliced crosswise
- Black Pepper, freshly ground
- Dijon Mustard, 1 teaspoon (5ml)
- Lemon Zest, from half a lemon
- Mayonnaise, ¼ cup (32 g)
- Garlic, minced, 1 clove
- Salt
- Lemon Juice, 1 tablespoon (15 ml) plus 1 teaspoon (5ml)
- Smoked Salmon, separated into strips, 8 oz. (0.23 kg),
- Chives, 2 tablespoons (30 ml), sliced

Procedure:

1. Mix pepper, mayonnaise, salt, garlic, Dijon mustard, lemon zest and juice in a small bowl and leave aside. Distribute the cucumber slices among four plates and top each with smoked salmon. Garnish with a little of the mayonnaise mixture and chives. Serve.

Nutritional Facts: Cal: 337; Carb: 3.7g; Protein: 22.4g; Fat: 25.1g; Fiber: 1.7g; Sugars: 3.3g; Cholesterol: 36mg; Sodium: 2200mg

11.6 Herbed Almond Roast

Serves: 5 Prep Time: 5 minutes Cook Time: 10 minutes

Ingredients:

- Coconut Oil. 2 tablespoons (30 ml)
- Rosemary Leaves, fresh, finely chopped, 2 teaspoons (10 ml)
- Salt
- Granulated Erythritol, 1 teaspoon (5ml)
- Dried Cumin Seed, ground, 1 teaspoon (5ml)
- Black Pepper, freshly ground
- Cayenne Pepper, 1 teaspoon (5ml)
- Raw Almonds, 1 ¼ cups (32 g)

Procedure:

1. In a large skillet over low heat, liquefy the oil. Toast the rosemary leaves and season with the salt, erythritol, cumin, black pepper and cayenne pepper. Stir together and toss in the almonds. Stir for about 30 seconds for 5 to 8 minutes until the almonds are roasted. Let cool before you serve.

Nutritional Facts: Cal: 300; Carb: 3.8g; Protein: 8.5g; Fat: 25.6g; Fiber: 5.2g; Sugars: 1.7g; Cholesterol: 0mg; Sodium: 469mg

11.7 Asparagus and Lemon Sesame Dressing

Serves: 4 Prep Time: 5 minutes Cook Time: 10 minutes

Ingredients:

- Asparagus Spears, trimmed, 16 pieces
- Avocado Oil, 3 tablespoons (45 ml)
- Tahini, 2 tablespoons (30 ml)
- Lemon Juice, 2 ½ teaspoons
- Garlic, minced, 1 small clove
- Salt
- Black Pepper, freshly ground
- Water, 1 ½ tablespoons

Procedure:

1. Over a medium temperature, place the asparagus and 2 tablespoons (30 ml) of avocado oil in a medium skillet. Allow to simmer for approximately 10 minutes, covering the asparagus spears in oil and rotating them until uniformly browned on all sides.
2. To make the sauce, whisk together water, pepper, salt, garlic, lemon juice, 1 tablespoon (15 ml) of avocado oil, and tahini in a small bowl. Use to season and serve cooked asparagus.

Nutritional Facts: Cal: 106; Carb: 2.9g; Protein: 3.5g; Fat: 7.7g; Fiber: 2.8g; Sugars: 2g; Cholesterol: 0mg; Sodium: 43mg

11.8 Cauliflower Sliders

Serves: 10 pieces Prep Time: 10 minutes Cook Time: 20 minutes

Ingredients:

- Black Pepper, freshly ground
- Cauliflower Rice, 3 cups (360 g)
- Garlic Powder, 1 teaspoon (5ml)
- Eggs, 2 large pieces
- Almond Meal, 2/3 cup
- Nutritional Yeast, ¼ cup (32 g)
- Chives, dried, 1 tablespoon (15 ml)
- Salt
- Turmeric, ground, ½ teaspoon (2.5 ml)
- Coconut Oil, 3 tablespoons (45 ml)

Procedure:

1. Place the cauliflower rice in a large saucepan and cover with enough water. Bring to a boil and let boil for 3 ½ minutes. Strain the cauliflower with a fine-mesh strainer and press to remove all the excess water.
2. Add the drained and cooked cauliflower into a large bowl and add the remainder of the ingredients except for the oil. Stir until well incorporated. Heat the oil in a large skillet over a medium flame. With a ¼ cup (32 g) scoop, shape the mixture into balls and place into the oil. Flatten with a spatula. Repeat to make 10 patties and cook for 5 minutes on each side or until browned. Serve immediately.

Nutritional Facts: Cal: 164; Carb: 3.3g; Protein: 6.6g; Fat: 12.3g; Fiber: 3.6g; Sugars: 2.9g; Cholesterol: 74mg; Sodium: 433mg

11.9 Buffalo Salami Chips

Serves: 6 Prep Time: 10 minutes Cook Time: 10 minutes

Ingredients:

- Turmeric Powder, 1 teaspoon (5ml)
- Garlic Powder, 1 ½ teaspoons (5.9 g)
- Onion Powder, 2 teaspoons (10 ml)
- Hot Sauce, 1 tablespoon (15 ml)
- Coconut Aminos, 1 tablespoon (15 ml)
- Nutritional Yeast, 1/3 cup (75 ml)
- Cooked Chicken, shredded, ¾ cup (175 ml)
- Coconut Milk, 1 cup (237 ml)
- Salami, 8 oz. (0.23 kg), sliced crosswise to make 24 pieces
- Salt
- Black Pepper, freshly ground
- Parsley Leaves, fresh, chopped, ¼ cup (32 g)

Procedure:

1. Heat up oven to 400 degrees Fahrenheit. Line two rimmed baking trays with a silpad or greaseproof parchment. Arrange the salami slices onto the trays and bake for 8-10 minutes until crisp.
2. Add the remainder of the ingredients except for the parsley into a saucepan and stir until well combined. Heat over a medium high flame and bring to a simmer. Lower to a medium low flame and allow to cook for 6 minutes, uncovered to let the sauce thicken. Serve with the baked salami chips.

Nutritional Facts: Cal: 294; Carb: 4.4g; Protein: 19.5g; Fat: 21.2g; Fiber: 2.1g; Sugars: 1.9g; Cholesterol: 54mg; Sodium: 830mg

11.10 Red and Green Chips and Dip

Serves: 2 Prep Time: 10 minutes, 12 hours to soak almonds Cook Time: 0 minutes

Ingredients:

- Basil Leaves, fresh, 1 cup (237 ml)
- Salt
- Raw Almonds, 1/3 cup (75 ml), soaked for 12 hours, rinsed and drained
- Lemon Juice, 1 ½ teaspoons (5.9 g)
- Parsley Leaves and Stems, fresh, 1/3 cup (75 ml)
- Garlic, 1 small clove
- Olive Oil, 2 tablespoons (30 ml)
- Cider Vinegar, 1 tablespoon (15 ml)
- Radishes, 20 medium pieces, thinly sliced

Procedure:

1. Add all of the ingredients except for the radishes into the jar of a food processor and blend on high until smooth. Pour the sauce into a bowl and serve with the radishes.

Nutritional Facts: Cal: 337; Carb: 4.8g; Protein: 8.1g; Fat: 29.4g; Fiber: 5.4g; Sugars: 2.4g; Cholesterol: 0mg; Sodium: 144mg

12 SAUCES AND ACCOMPANIMENTS

12.1 Mayonnaise

Serves: 1 ¼ cup (32 g) s Prep Time: 5 minutes
Cook Time: 0 minutes

Ingredients:

- Black Pepper, freshly ground
- Olive Oil, 1 cup (237 ml)
- Dijon Mustard, 1 teaspoon (5ml)
- Egg, 1 large
- Lemon Juice, 1 tablespoon (15 ml)
- Egg Yolks, 2 large yolks
- Cider Vinegar, 1 tablespoon (15 ml)
- Salt

Procedure:

1. Add all of the ingredients into a blender jar except for the oil. Pulse until the ingredients are well combined. Set the blender on medium speed and slowly add the oil in a thin stream over 2 minutes. Once the oil has been added, continue to blend until it resembles mayonnaise.

Nutritional Facts: Cal: 200; Carb: 0.3g; Protein: 1.2g; Fat: 21.6g; Fiber: 0g; Sugars: 0g; Cholesterol: 61mg; Sodium: 62mg

12.2 Quick Fire Barbecue Sauce

Serves: 1 ¼ cup (32 g) s Prep Time: 5 minutes
Cook Time: 0 minutes

Ingredients:

- Balsamic Vinegar, ¼ cup (32 g)
- Water, 1/3 cup (75 ml)
- Black Pepper, freshly ground
- Tomato Paste, 1 (6 oz.) can
- Spanish Paprika, ½ teaspoon (2.5 ml)
- Garlic Powder, ½ teaspoon (2.5 ml)
- Onion Powder, ½ teaspoon (2.5 ml)
- Dijon Mustard, 1 tablespoon (15 ml)
- Coconut Aminos, 2 tablespoons (30 ml)
- Salt

Procedure:

1. Add all of the ingredients into a large airtight container and shake until fully incorporated. Use within 5 days.

Nutritional Facts: Cal: 11; Carb: 1.7g; Protein: 0.4g; Fat: 0.1g; Fiber: 0.4g; Sugars: 1.1g; Cholesterol: 0mg; Sodium: 66mg

12.3 Thai Vegetable Dressing

Serves: 1 cup (237 ml) Prep Time: 5 minutes
Cook Time: 0 minutes

Ingredients:

- Salt
- Cayenne Pepper, ½ teaspoon
- Garlic Powder, 1 teaspoon (5ml)
- Lime Juice, 1 tablespoon (15 ml)
- Sesame Oil, toasted, 2 tablespoons (30 ml)
- Coconut Aminos, 2 tablespoons (30 ml)
- Cider Vinegar, 2 tablespoons (30 ml)
- Coconut Milk, ¼ cup (32 g)
- Almond Butter, unsweetened, ¼ cup (32 g)

Procedure:

1. Add all of the ingredients into a large airtight container and shake until fully incorporated. When ready to use, shake container before the dressing is drizzled.

Nutritional Facts: Cal: 22; Carb: 0.6g; Protein: 0.1g; Fat: 2g; Fiber: 0.1g; Sugars: 0.1g; Cholesterol: 0mg; Sodium: 61mg

12.4 Vegan Sour Cream and Chive Dip

Serves: 1 cup (237 ml) Prep Time: 5 minutes, plus 12 hours to soak cashews Cook Time: 0

Ingredients:

- Garlic Powder, ¼ teaspoon (1.25 ml)
- Onion Powder, ¾ teaspoon
- Salt
- Nutritional Yeast, 2 teaspoons (10 ml)
- Cider Vinegar, 2 tablespoons (30 ml)
- Dairy-Free Yogurt, Unsweetened, ¼ cup (32 g)
- Raw Cashew Nuts, 1 cup (237 ml)
- Chives, fresh, 2 tablespoons (30 ml), sliced

Procedure:

1. Soak the cashews in a 12 oz., container filled with water. Store in the refrigerator for 12 hours. Once softened, drain from the water and add into the jar of a blender along with the remainder of the ingredients except the chives. Blend on a high setting until smooth. Transfer into an airtight container and stir in the chives. Leave to sit for an hour for flavours to develop.

Nutritional Facts: Cal: 55; Carb: 2.7g; Protein: 1.5g; Fat: 4.1g; Fiber: 0.5g; Sugars: 0.5g; Cholesterol: 0mg; Sodium: 62mg

12.5 Homemade Ranch Dressing

Serves: 2 cups (64 g)Prep Time: 5 minutes Cook Time: 0 minutes

Ingredients:

- Black Pepper, freshly ground
- Salt
- Lemon Juice, 1 tablespoon (15 ml)
- Cider Vinegar, 1 tablespoon (15 ml)
- Dill Weed, fresh, finely chopped, 1 tablespoon (15 ml)
- Onions, White, minced, 1 tablespoon (15 ml)
- Garlic, minced, 2 small cloves
- Chives, fresh, sliced, 2 tablespoons (30 ml)
- Parsley Leaves, fresh, finely chopped, 3 tablespoons (45 ml)
- Coconut Milk, ½ cup (118 ml)
- Mayonnaise, 1 cup (237 ml) (see recipe in this chapter)

Procedure:

1. Add all of the ingredients into a 12 oz. jar and seal tightly, Shake all of the ingredients until fully incorporated. Shake the container before every use.

Nutritional Facts: Cal: 57; Carb: 0.3g; Protein: 0.1g; Fat: 6.1g; Fiber: 0.1g; Sugars: 0.1g; Cholesterol: 7mg; Sodium: 182mg

12.6 Home-made Honey Mustard Dressing

Serves: 1 ¾ cups Prep Time: 5 minutes Cook Time: 0 minutes

Ingredients:

- Honey, 1 tablespoon (15 ml) plus 1 teaspoon (5ml)
- Lemon Juice, 2 tablespoons (30 ml)
- Dijon Mustard, ¼ cup (32 g)
- Cider Vinegar, ¼ cup (32 g)
- Olive Oil, 1 cup (237 ml)
- Salt

Procedure:

1. Add all of the ingredients into an 18 oz. jar or container and shake until fully incorporated. Shake the jar before every use.

Nutritional Facts: Cal: 74; Carb: 1g; Protein: 0.1g; Fat: 7.9g; Fiber: 0.1g; Sugars: 0.9g; Cholesterol: 0mg; Sodium: 61mg

12.7 Green Goddess Goodness

Serves: 1 ½ cups (350 ml) Prep Time: 5 minutes
Cook Time: 0 minutes

Ingredients:

- Dijon Mustard, 2 teaspoons (10 ml)
- Olive Oil, ½ cup (118 ml)
- Mayonnaise, ½ cup (118 ml) (see recipe in this Chapter)
- Cider Vinegar, 3 tablespoons (45 ml)
- Tarragon Leaves, dried, ½ teaspoon (2.5 ml)
- Chives, dried, 2 tablespoons (30 ml)
- Coconut Aminos, 2 teaspoons (10 ml)
- Garlic Powder, 1 teaspoon (5ml)
- Parsley Leaves, dried, 2 teaspoons (10 ml)
- Distilled White Vinegar, 1 teaspoon (5ml)
- Salt

Procedure:

1. Add all of the ingredients into a 16 oz. jar or container and shake until fully incorporated. Shake the jar before every use.

Nutritional Facts: Cal: 75; Carb: 0.2g; Protein: 0.1g; Fat: 8.2g; Fiber: 0g; Sugars: 0g; Cholesterol: 2mg; Sodium: 45mg

12.8 Bacon Vinaigrette

Serves: ½ cup (118 ml) Prep Time: 2 minutes
Cook Time: 0 minutes

Ingredients:

- Rendered Bacon Fat, 1/3 cup (75 ml)
- Lemon Juice, 3 tablespoons (45 ml)
- Salt
- Black Pepper, freshly ground

Procedure:

1. Add all of the ingredients into a 7 oz. jar or container and shake until fully incorporated. If stored, let the jar sit out to let the bacon fat liquefy, then shake the jar before every use.

Nutritional Facts: Cal: 79; Carb: 0.2g; Protein: 0.1g; Fat: 8.6g; Fiber: 0g; Sugars: 0.1g; Cholesterol: 8mg; Sodium: 60mg

12.9 Teriyaki Sauce

Serves: 1 ½ cups (350 ml) Prep Time: 5 minutes
Cook Time: 0 minutes

Ingredients:

- Salt
- Olive Oil, 1 cup (237 ml)
- Ginger, ground, 1 teaspoon (5ml)
- Garlic Powder, 1 teaspoon (5ml)
- Cider Vinegar, 1 tablespoon (15 ml)
- Coconut Aminos, ¼ cup (32 g)
- Erythritol. 2 tablespoons (30 ml)

Procedure:

1. Add all of the ingredients into a 16 oz. jar or container and shake until fully incorporated. Shake the jar before every use.

Nutritional Facts: Cal: 85; Carb: 0.7g; Protein: 0g; Fat: 9.1g; Fiber: 0g; Sugars: 0g; Cholesterol: 0mg; Sodium: 81mg

12.10 Quick Fire Hollandaise Sauce

Serves: 1 ¾ cups Prep Time: 2 minutes Cook Time: 0 minutes

Ingredients:

- Ghee, 1 ¼ cup (32 g)s, solidified
- Egg Yolks, 6 large yolks
- Lemon Juice, 2 tablespoons (30 ml)
- Salt
- Cayenne Pepper, a pinch

Procedure:

1. Add all of the ingredients into the jar of a food processor and blend on medium for 15 to 25 seconds until the sauce has fully emulsified. Use immediately or store in an airtight container. Before each use, let sauce return to room temperature then transfer to a food processor to blend once more before sauce is used.

Nutritional Facts: Cal: 100; Carb: 0.2g; Protein: 0.6g; Fat: 10.7g; Fiber: 0g; Sugars: 0g; Cholesterol: 45mg; Sodium: 68mg

13 SMOOTHIES AND DRINKS

13.1 Ketogenic Electrolyte Booster

Serves: 1 liter Prep Time: 10 minutes Cook Time: 0 minutes

Ingredients:

- Black Tea, brewed, 4 cups
- Lemon Juice, ¼ cup (32 g)
- Erythritol, 2 teaspoons (10 ml)
- Salt, ½ teaspoon (2.5 ml)

Procedure:

1. Add all of the ingredients into a large pitcher that can hold up to a liter of liquid, and stir with a large spoon until fully combined.

Nutritional Facts: Cal: 6; Carb: 0.6g; Protein: 0.2g; Fat: 0.2g; Fiber: 0.1g; Sugars: 0.6g; Cholesterol: 0mg; Sodium: 376mg

13.2 Turmeric Ginger Coolers

Serves: 750 mL Prep Time: 5 minutes Cook Time: 5 minutes

Ingredients:

- Ginger, ground, 1 teaspoon (5ml)
- Turmeric, ground, 1 teaspoon (5ml)
- Lemon Juice, ¼ cup (32 g)
- Aloe Vera, 2 teaspoons (10 ml)
- Erythritol, 2 teaspoons (10 ml)
- Salt
- Black Pepper, freshly ground
- Mint Leaves, 6 leaves
- Water, 2 ½ cups
- Lemon Wedges, 6 small pieces

Procedure:

1. In a large saucepan, bring the water, ginger, and turmeric to a rolling boil. Remove from the heat and stir in the lemon juice, aloe Vera, erythritol, salt, and black pepper. Stir until completely dissolved, then set aside to cool for one hour. In a large pitcher, combine the lemon wedges and mint leaves with the remaining ingredients. Chill till cold. Before consuming, the herbs may be strained.

Nutritional Facts: Cal: 13; Carb: 1.5g; Protein: 0.4g; Fat: 0.4g; Fiber: 0.5g; Sugars: 0.7g; Cholesterol: 0mg; Sodium: 204mg

13.3 Old-Fashioned Egg Cream

Serves: 1 Prep Time: 1 minutes Cook Time: 0 minutes

Ingredients:

- Milk, non-dairy or regular, 3 tablespoons (45 ml)
- Cocoa Powder, 2 teaspoons (10 ml)
- Erythritol, ½ teaspoon (2.5 ml)
- Sparkling Water, 12 oz., chilled

Procedure:

1. Whisk the milk, cocoa powder and erythritol together in a large glass until fully incorporated. Slowly add the chilled, sparkling water. Serve immediately.

Nutritional Facts: Cal: 22; Carb: 0.9g; Protein: 0.9g; Fat: 1.1g; Fiber: 1.2g; Sugars: 0g; Cholesterol: 0mg; Sodium: 1mg

13.4 Vanilla Smoothie

Serves: 1 8 oz. serving Prep Time: 2 minutes Cook Time: 0 minutes

Ingredients:

- Ice Cubes, 4
- Water, ½ cup (118 ml)
- Vanilla Extract, ½ teaspoon (2.5 ml)
- Protein Powder, 2 tablespoons (30 ml)
- Erythritol, 1 teaspoon (5ml)
- Coconut Oil, 1 tablespoon (15 ml)
- Almond Butter, unsweetened, smooth, 1 tablespoon (15 ml)
- Egg Yolk, 1 large

Procedure:

1. Add all of the ingredients to a blender jar and blend for 30 seconds on high until completely combined. Immediately pour into a glass and serve.

Nutritional Facts: Cal: 283; Carb: 2.3g; Protein: 6.1g; Fat: 27.1g; Fiber: 1.6g; Sugars: 1.1g; Cholesterol: 210mg; Sodium: 9mg

13.5 Chai Smoothie

Serves: 1 16 oz., serving Prep Time: 10 minutes Cook Time: 0 minutes

Ingredients:

- Chai Tea, 1 teabag, regular or decaffeinated
- Boiling Water, 1 cup (237 ml)
- MCT Oil Powder, unflavored, 2 tablespoons (30 ml)
- Protein Powder, 2 tablespoons (30 ml)
- Erythritol, 1 ½ teaspoons (5.9 g)
- Ice Cubes, 6 pieces
- Milk, non-dairy or regular, ½ cup (118 ml)

Procedure:

1. Steep the tea in boiling water in a large mug for 10 to 15 minutes. While this steeps, add the MCT Oil Powder, Protein Powder and Erythritol into a blender jar. Add the steeped tea and blend on high for 30 seconds until well incorporated. Pour the ice cubes into a glass and pour in the tea mix. Pour milk on top to serve.

Nutritional Facts: Cal: 217; Carb: 1.5g; Protein: 12g; Fat: 14g; Fiber: 2g; Sugars: 0g; Cholesterol: 0mg; Sodium: 58mg

13.6 Spring Clean Smoothie

Serves: 2 Prep Time: 5 minutes Cook Time: 0 minutes

Ingredients:

- Non-dairy Milk, 1 cup (237 ml)
- Zucchini, frozen then chopped, ¾ cup
- Avocado, pitted, peeled and sliced, ½ medium piece
- Spinach, 1 handful
- Protein Powder, 2 tablespoons (30 ml)
- Coconut Oil, 1 tablespoon (15 ml)
- Matcha Powder, ¾ teaspoon

Procedure:

1. Add all the ingredients to a blender and process for 30 to 40 seconds, or until smooth. Quickly divide into two glasses and serve.

Nutritional Facts: Cal: 200; Carb: 7.3g; Protein: 10.6g; Fat: 14.3g; Fiber: 3.3g; Sugars: 2.7g; Cholesterol: 0mg; Sodium: 131mg

13.7 Matcha Cream Smoothie

Serves: 1 8 oz., glass Prep Time: 5 minutes Cook Time: 0 minutes

Ingredients:

- Milk, non-dairy or regular, ½ cup (118 ml)
- Matcha Powder, 2 teaspoons (10 ml)
- Ice Cream, regular or dairy-free, 4 scoops

Procedure:

1. Add the milk and matcha into a large sealable container and whisk until the matcha has fully dissolved. Add the ice cream into the container and cover. Shake for 20 to 30 seconds. Remove the lid and add a straw. Serve immediately.

Nutritional Facts: Cal: 193; Carb: 15.5g; Protein: 1.5g; Fat: 14g; Fiber: 17.5g; Sugars: 2.5g; Cholesterol: 0mg; Sodium: 185mg

13.8 Tropical Strawberry Smoothie

Serves: 2 8 oz. glasses Prep Time: 5 minutes Cook Time: 0 minutes

Ingredients:

- Strawberries, hulled, 6 oz.,
- Water, 2/3 cup
- Coconut Milk, frozen into cubes, ½ cup (118 ml)
- Vanilla Extract, ½ teaspoon (2.5 ml)

Procedure:

1. Add all of the ingredients into the jar of a blender and process on high for 40 to 50 seconds until the coconut milk cubes have been broken down and the shake is smooth. Pour into glasses and serve immediately.

Nutritional Facts: Cal: 121; Carb: 5.5g; Protein: 1.1g; Fat: 9.8g; Fiber: 1.7g; Sugars: 4.3g; Cholesterol: 0mg; Sodium: 1mg

13.9 Coconut Soda

Serves: 1 16 oz. Glass Prep Time: 1 minute Cook Time: 0 minutes

Ingredients:

- Coconut Milk, 1/3 cup (75 ml)
- Liquid Stevia, 3 drops
- Sparkling Water, chilled, 12 oz.

Procedure:

1. Pour the coconut milk into a tall glass and stir in the stevia until well combined. Pour the sparkling water and serve.

Nutritional Facts: Cal: 116; Carb: 1g; Protein: 1g; Fat: 12g; Fiber: 0g; Sugars: 1g; Cholesterol: 0mg; Sodium: 25mg

13.10 Red-Eye Wide-Eye Shake

Serves: 1 14 oz. serving Prep Time: 5 minutes Cook Time: 0 minutes

Ingredients:

- Coconut Milk, 1 cup (237 ml)
- Water, ½ cup (118 ml)
- Ice Cubes, 4 pieces
- Coconut Oil, 2 tablespoons (30 ml)
- Cocoa Powder, 1 ½ tablespoons
- Liquid Stevia, 2 drops
- Instant Coffee, ½ teaspoon (2.5 ml)

Procedure:

1. Add all of the ingredients into the jar of a blender. Blend on high until the ice has broken up and the shake is smooth. Transfer into a glass and serve.

Nutritional Facts: Cal: 757; Carb: 9.6g; Protein: 6.1g; Fat: 76g; Fiber: 2.7g; Sugars: 4g; Cholesterol: 0mg; Sodium: 60mg

13.11 Earthy Coffee Shake

Serves: 1 12 oz. serving Prep Time: 1 minute
Cook Time: 0 minutes

Ingredients:

- Brewed Coffee, hot, decaffeinated or regular, 1 ¼ cup (32 g)s
- Protein Powder, 2 tablespoons (30 ml)
- Coconut Oil, 2 tablespoons (30 ml)
- Liquid Stevia, 2 drops
- Coconut Milk, 2 tablespoons (30 ml)
- Exogenous Ketones, ½ teaspoon (2.5 ml)
- Vanilla Extract, ¼ teaspoon (1.25 ml)
- Cordyceps fungi, 0.1 ounce (optional)

Procedure:

1. Add all of the ingredients into the jar of a blender and blend on high for 20 to 30 seconds until fully incorporated. Transfer into a glass and serve immediately.

Nutritional Facts: Cal: 334; Carb: 0.4g; Protein: 18.5g; Fat: 28.8g; Fiber: 0g; Sugars: 0.3g; Cholesterol: 0mg; Sodium: 224mg

13.12 Chocolate Booster Shake

Serves: 2 10 oz. servings Prep Time: 5 minutes
Cook Time: 0 minutes

Ingredients:

- Coconut Butter, 1 tablespoon (15 ml)
- Liquid Stevia, 4 drops
- Coconut Oil, 2 tablespoons (30 ml)
- Protein Powder, 2 tablespoons (30 ml)
- Cocoa Powder, 2 tablespoons (30 ml)
- Milk, hot, non-dairy or regular, 2 cups (475 ml)
- Cinnamon, ground, 1 pinch

Procedure:

- Add all of the ingredients into the jar of a blender and blend on high for 10 seconds until fully incorporated. Transfer into two mugs and sprinkle with cinnamon. Serve immediately.

Nutritional Facts: Cal: 357; Carb: 6.9g; Protein: 12.5g; Fat: 29.3g; Fiber: 4.1g; Sugars: 1.1g; Cholesterol: 0mg; Sodium: 144mg

13.13 Watermelon Coolers

Serves: 4 4 oz. servings Prep Time: 5 minutes Cook Time: 0 minutes

Ingredients:

- Watermelon, cubed, fresh, 4.5 oz.,
- Mint Leaves, 12 pieces
- Ice Cubes, 8 pieces
- Lime Juice, 4 teaspoons
- Sparkling Water, 1 1/8 cups.

Procedure:

1. Prepare four glasses and portion the diced watermelon, 3 mint leaves, 2 ice cubes and a teaspoon of lime juice for each glass. Mash the remainder of the watermelon cubes to extract their juice and portion 2 teaspoons (10 ml) per glass. Top with the sparkling water per glass and serve immediately.

Nutritional Facts: Cal: 70; Carb: 1.3g; Protein: 0.1g; Fat: 0g; Fiber: 0g; Sugars: 0.6g; Cholesterol: 0mg; Sodium: 2mg

13.14 Virgin Margaritas

Serves: 4 8 oz. servings Prep Time: 5 minutes Cook Time: 0 minutes

Ingredients:

- Salt, 2 tablespoons (30 ml)
- Lime Wedge, 1 piece
- Ice Cubes, 4 cups
- Lime Juice, ½ cup (118 ml)
- Liquid Stevia, 6 drops
- Lime Wedges to garnish

Procedure:

1. Prepare the glasses and line their rims with salt. To do this, place the salt on a saucer and moisten the edges of each glass with the lime wedge. Place the edge of the glass on the saucer with the salt and rotate to coat. Place the remainder of the ingredients except the lime wedges in a blender and blend on high to form a slush. Portion into the prepared glasses and serve with a lime wedge.

Nutritional Facts: Cal: 77; Carb: 2g; Protein: 0.1g; Fat: 0.1g; Fiber: 0.1g; Sugars: 0.4g; Cholesterol: 0mg; Sodium: 3501mg

14 DESSERTS

14.1 Chocolate Soft-Serve

Serves: 4 Prep Time: 10 minutes plus 30-45 minutes to freeze Cook Time: 0 minutes

Ingredients:

- Coconut Milk, 1 (13.5 oz.) can
- Protein Powder, ¼ cup (32 g)
- Almond Butter, smooth and unsweetened, 2 tablespoons (30 ml)
- Cocoa Powder, 2 tablespoons (30 ml)
- Liquid Stevia, 3 drops
- Vanilla Extract, 1 teaspoon (5ml)

Procedure:

1. Add all of the ingredients into a blender jar or a food processor bowl and blend until fully incorporated. Portion into four bowls and set in the freezer to let the ice cream solidify. After 30 minutes, take each bowl and break it up with a fork to ensure it does not become a solid mass. If still soft, leave for 15 more minutes and break it up. Serve immediately.

Nutritional Facts: Cal: 478; Carb: 4.4g; Protein: 5.8g; Fat: 46.6g; Fiber: 4.6g; Sugars: 3.4g; Cholesterol: 0mg; Sodium: 13mg

14.2 Blueberries and Cream Crumble

Serves: 6 Prep Time: 5 minutes Cook Time: 25 minutes

Ingredients:

- Coconut Cream, 1 cup (237 ml)
- Cinnamon, ground, 1 teaspoon (5ml)
- Coconut Flour, 2 tablespoons (30 ml)
- Coconut Oil, 1/3 cup (75 ml)
- Blueberries, fresh or frozen, 18 oz.,
- Almond Meal, blanched, 1 cup (237 ml)
- Erythritol, 1/3 cup (75 ml)

Procedure:

1. Heat up an oven to 350 degrees Fahrenheit. Spread the blueberries in a single layer in an 8 inch baking dish. Whisk together the Almond Meal, coconut oil, erythritol, coconut flour and cinnamon in a small bowl to form the crumble base. Sprinkle on top of the prepared blueberries and bake in the heated oven for 22 to 25 minutes until golden brown.

2. Remove from the oven and let cool. Portion into 6 pieces and top with 2 to 3 tablespoons (45 ml) of the coconut cream.

Nutritional Facts: Cal: 388; Carb: 12.7g; Protein: 4.9g; Fat: 33.4g; Fiber: 4.3g; Sugars: 9.1g; Cholesterol: 0mg; Sodium: 1mg

14.3 Strawberry Shortcake Granita

Serves: 4 Prep Time: 5 minutes Cook Time: 0 minutes

Ingredients:

- Strawberries, hulled, fresh or frozen, 9 pieces
- Coconut Cream, 1/3 cup (75 ml)
- Cider Vinegar, 1 tablespoon (15 ml)
- Liquid Stevia, 2 drops
- Ice Cubes, 3 cups (360 g)

Procedure:

1. Add all of the ingredients except for the ice cubes into a blender jar or food processor bowl and blend until fully incorporated and smooth. Add the ice cubes and pulse until the ice is crushed. Portion into bowls and serve immediately.

Nutritional Facts: Cal: 61g; Carb: 2.3; Protein: 0.7g; Fat: 5g; Fiber: 1g; Sugars: 2g; Cholesterol: 0mg; Sodium: 4mg

14.4 Five-Layered Dessert Bars

Serves: 12 Prep Time: 20 minutes Cook Time: 35 minutes

Ingredients:

- Baking Powder, ¼ teaspoon (1.25 ml)
- Egg, 1 large
- Salt, ¼ teaspoon (1.25 ml)
- Butter, liquefied, 2 tablespoons (30 ml)
- Almonds, chopped, 1 cup (237 ml)
- Almond Meal, 1 cup (237 ml)
- Chocolate Chips, Stevia-Sweetened, 2 cups (475 ml)
- Walnuts, chopped, 1 cup (237 ml)
- Unsweetened Coconut, shredded, 1 cup (237 ml)

Procedure:

1. Heat up an oven to 300 degrees Fahrenheit and grease an 8"x8" dish with butter,
2. Mix together the Almond Meal, salt, and baking powder until fully incorporated. Stir in the egg and liquefied butter until well mixed. Pout into the prepared baking dish and press down with a spatula. Bake for 20 minutes in the oven and remove.
3. Increase the oven temperature to 350 degrees Fahrenheit and spread a cup of the chocolate chips onto the top of the dish. Sprinkle walnuts and almonds on top. Add the remainder of the chocolate chips and top with the coconut. Bake for 10 minutes or until the chocolate has liquefied.
4. Remove and let cool. Serve or store for up to a week in the refrigerator.

Nutritional Facts: Cal: 313; Carb: 6g; Protein: 6g; Fat: 21g; Fiber: 4g; Sugars: 11g; Cholesterol: 25mg; Sodium: 67mg

14.5 Home-Made Chewies

Serves: 8 (1 piece per serving) Prep Time: 10 minutes plus 30 minutes to set Cook Time: 5 minutes

Ingredients:

- Lemon Juice, ½ cup (118 ml)
- Strawberries, fresh or frozen, 8 pieces
- Gelatin, unflavored, 2 tablespoons (30 ml)
- Exogenous Ketones, 2 teaspoons (10 ml)

Procedure:

1. Prepare a silicone mold or greaseproof parchment-lined metal baking dish and set aside. Add the lemon juice, strawberries, and gelatin to the bowl of a food processor and process until thoroughly combined. Pour the mixture into a small saucepan and heat over a low flame for five minutes, or until it becomes liquid. Remove the mixture from the heat and whisk in the ketones. Pour the mixture into the silicone mold or prepared baking dish and chill for half an hour. Serve.

Nutritional Facts: Cal: 19; Carb: 0.9g; Protein: 3.2g; Fat: 0.2g; Fiber: 0.3g; Sugars: 0.9g; Cholesterol: 0mg; Sodium: 10mg

14.6 Meringue Cookies

Serves: 12, 2 per serving Prep Time: 10 minutes plus 1 hr. to cool Cook Time: 1 hour

Ingredients:

- Egg Whites, room temperature, from 2 eggs
- Cream of Tartar, ¼ teaspoon (1.25 ml)
- Salt, a pinch
- Confectioners' Erythritol, ½ cup (118 ml)
- Vanilla Extract, ½ teaspoon (2.5 ml)
- Strawberries, fresh, sliced, 24 pieces
- Coconut Cream, ¾ cup (175 ml)
- Mint Leaves, 12 pieces

Procedure:

1. Pre-heat the oven to 225°F. Prepare a baking sheet by covering it with silicone or greaseproof paper.
2. Into a clean bowl, add the egg whites, cream of tartar and salt and mix on a low speed until the egg whites foam. Once it foams, increase the speed to high and slowly add the erythritol, a tablespoon at a time, every 20 seconds until the mixture thickens and becomes glossy. The egg whites should have doubled in volume. Fold in the vanilla extract.
3. Dollop the meringues onto the prepared sheet to make a dozen. Bake for an hour with the oven door closed. After an hour, switch off the heat but leave the meringues to cool in the oven. Serve 2 pieces per plate and garnish with 4 strawberry slices, 2 tablespoons (30 ml) of coconut cream and 2 mint leaves.

Nutritional Facts: Cal: 100; Carb: 4g; Protein: 2.3g; Fat: 7.6g; Fiber: 1.8g; Sugars: 3.5g; Cholesterol: 0mg; Sodium: 56mg

14.7 Coconut Macaroons

Serves: 20 pieces, 2 per serving Prep Time: 10 minutes, 45 minutes to chill Cook Time: 5 minutes

Ingredients:

- Erythritol, ½ cup (118 ml)
- Coconut Milk, ¼ cup (32 g)
- Coconut Oil, 3 tablespoons (45 ml)
- Cocoa Powder, ¼ cup (32 g)
- Shredded Coconut, unsweetened, 2 cups (400 g)

Procedure:

1. Use silicone baking mats or greaseproof paper to line a baking pan.
2. Mix the erythritol, coconut milk, and coconut oil in a large skillet. Whisk for around 5 minutes as the mixture comes to a simmer over a medium-low temperature.
3. Once it simmers, stir in the cocoa powder, and then the shredded coconut. Scoop the mixture using a tablespoonful measure onto the prepared cookie sheet. Repeat to make 20 cookies. Chill for 30 to 45 minutes until set. Serve.

Nutritional Facts: Cal: 122; Carb: 4.2g; Protein: 1.3g; Fat: 11.9g; Fiber: 2.5g; Sugars: 1.2g; Cholesterol: 0mg; Sodium: 4mg

14.8 Chocolate Almond Butter Balls

Serves: 8 Prep Time: 10 minutes Cook Time: 0 minutes, 1 hour to freeze

Ingredients:

- Almond Butter, creamy and sugar-free, 1 1/3 cups (367 g)
- Vanilla Extract, 2 teaspoons (10 ml)
- Cocoa Powder, unsweetened, 2 tablespoons (30 ml)
- Shredded Coconut, unsweetened, 2 cups (400 g)
- Coconut Oil, 2 tablespoons (30 ml)

Procedure:

1. Line a cookie sheet with greaseproof parchment or a silpad.
2. In a large bowl, whisk together all of the ingredients until fully incorporated. Portion into 8 pieces and scoop onto the prepared sheet. Press flat and allow to freeze for an hour to let set. Serve, or store for up to a week.

Nutritional Facts: Cal: 361; Carb: 4.5g; Protein: 10g; Fat: 32g; Fiber: 4.5g; Sugars: 1g; Cholesterol: 0mg; Sodium: 186mg

14.9 Almond Spice Cookies

Serves: 12 Prep Time: 10 minutes Cook Time: 15 minutes

Ingredients:

- Almond Meal, blanched, 2 cups (400 g)
- Cinnamon, ground, 1 teaspoon (5ml)
- Butter, softened, ½ cup (118 ml)
- Almond Extract, 1/8 teaspoon (0.6g)
- Egg, 1 large
- Erythritol, granulated, ½ cup (118 ml)
- Vanilla Extract, 1 teaspoon (5ml)

Procedure:

1. Heat up an oven to 350 degrees Fahrenheit. Prepare a cookie sheet with a silicone pad or greaseproof parchment and set aside.
2. Mix all of the ingredients in a large bowl until they are fully incorporated. Roll into 1 inch balls and set on the prepared sheet. Flatten with a fork and bake for 12 minutes or until golden. Let cool before you remove from the sheet. Serve immediately or store.

Nutritional Facts: Cal: 150; Carb: 4.5g; Protein: 2.5g; Fat: 8g; Fiber: 0.5g; Sugars: 0g; Cholesterol: 36mg; Sodium: 7mg

14.10 Home-Made Chocolate Peanut Butter Morsels

Serves: 12 Prep Time: 10 minutes Cook Time: 10 minutes plus 1 hour to freeze

Ingredients:

- Coconut Oil, 1 cup (237 ml)
- Peanut Butter, creamy and sugar-free, ½ cup (118 ml)
- Coconut Cream, 2 tablespoons (30 ml)
- Cocoa Powder, 1 tablespoon (15 ml)
- Erythritol, granulated, 1/3 cup (75 ml)
- Vanilla Extract, ¼ teaspoon (1.25 ml)
- Salt, 1/8 teaspoon (0.6g)
- Peanuts, roasted, 2 tablespoons (30 ml)

Procedure:

1. Line a cupcake tin with liners and set aside. Liquefy the coconut oil over low heat in a saucepan. Add the peanut butter and stir until dissolved. Whisk the remainder of the ingredients into the mixture. Pour into the prepared tin and freeze for an hour. Serve or store in a resealable bag for up to a week.

Nutritional Facts: Cal: 230; Carb: 5.5g; Protein: 2.5g; Fat: 24g; Fiber: 0.5g; Sugars: 1g; Cholesterol: 0mg; Sodium: 71mg

14.11 Pumpkin Cheesecakes

Serves: 12 Prep Time: 10 minutes Cook Time: 40 minutes

Ingredients:

- Vanilla Extract, 1 teaspoon (5ml)
- Cream Cheese, 1 package, softened
- Pumpkin Puree, 1 cup (237 ml)
- Eggs, 5 large, room temperature
- Erythritol, granulated, 1 cup (237 ml)
- Pumpkin Spice, 1 teaspoon (5ml)
- Cinnamon, ground, 1 teaspoon (5ml)

Procedure:

1. Heat up an oven to 350 degrees Fahrenheit. Grease an 8" x 8" baking tray with butter and set aside.
2. Combine the pumpkin puree with the cream cheese and beat until combined. Combine the remaining ingredients by stirring continuously. After preheating the oven, pour the mixture into the prepared dish and bake for 40 minutes. Allow it cool, then cut into bars and serve. You may keep it in a bag in the fridge for up to a week.

Nutritional Facts: Cal: 96; Carb: 1.5g; Protein: 4g; Fat: 8g; Fiber: 0g; Sugars: 1g; Cholesterol: 85mg; Sodium: 97mg

14.12 Guilt-Free Cookie Dough

Serves: 8 Prep Time: 5 minutes Cook Time: 0 minutes

Ingredients:

- Heavy Cream, ½ cup (118 ml)
- Coconut Cream, ¼ cup (32 g)
- Erythritol, granulated, ½ cup (118 ml)
- Coconut Flour, ¾ cup (175 ml)
- Butter, liquefied, ¾ cup (175 ml)
- Vanilla Extract, 1 teaspoon (5ml)
- Salt, ¼ teaspoon (1.25 ml)
- Chocolate Chips, stevia-sweetened, 1/3 cup (75 ml)

Procedure:

1. In a large bowl, mix everything but the chocolate chips. The chocolate chips should be added last and mixed together thoroughly. Divide among 8 bowls, serve immediately, or refrigerate for up to 7 days.

Nutritional Facts: Cal: 266; Carb: 16g; Protein: 2g; Fat: 26g; Fiber: 7g; Sugars: 3g; Cholesterol: 45mg; Sodium: 81mg

14.13 Lemon Curd Tart

Serves: 8 Prep Time: 15 minutes Cook Time: 10 minutes plus 4 hours to freeze

Ingredients:

- Butter, 8 tablespoons plus ¼ cup (32 g)
- Lemon Extract, 1 teaspoon (5ml)
- Coconut Flour, ¾ cup (175 ml)
- Eggs, 2 large
- Lemon Zest, 2 teaspoons (10 ml)
- Heavy Cream, 1 cup (237 ml)
- Egg Yolks, 4 pieces
- Lemon Juice, 1/3 cup (75 ml)
- Erythritol, powdered, ½ cup (118 ml)
- Sour Cream, 1 cup (237 ml)

Procedure:

1. Make the base of the crust by cutting together the 8 tablespoons butter into the coconut flour with a fork or pastry cutter. Press the mixture onto the base of a pie tin or tart mold and set aside.
2. Whisk the zest, juice, yolks, eggs, and cream together in a large saucepan over a medium low temperature for 5 minutes, or until the mixture begins to thicken. Take off the burner and mix in the 1/4 cup of butter, the lemon extract, and the erythritol until the sugar is dissolved. Blend the sour cream in thoroughly by stirring.
3. When the crust has been prepared, pour the filling into it and place it in the refrigerator for 4 hours to set. Keep in the fridge for up to a week before serving or storing.

Nutritional Facts: Cal: 369; Carb: 0g; Protein: 5g; Fat: 37g; Fiber: 6g; Sugars: 1.5g; Cholesterol: 251mg; Sodium: 138mg

14.14 Chocolate Tart

Serves: 8 Prep Time: 30 minutes Cook Time: 20 minutes plus 2 hours to freeze

Ingredients:

- Almond Meal, 1 ¼ cup (32 g)s
- Unsweetened Coconut, shredded, ¾ cup (175 ml)
- Egg, 1 large
- Coconut Oil, ¼ cup (32 g)
- Coconut Cream, ¾ cup (175 ml)
- Erythritol, granulated, 1/3 cup (75 ml)
- Cocoa Powder, 2 tablespoons (30 ml)
- Vanilla Extract, 1 teaspoon (5ml)
- Salt, 1/8 teaspoon (0.6g)

Procedure:

1. Heat up an oven to 350 degrees Fahrenheit. Line a 9 inch pie tin with greaseproof parchment and set aside.
2. Make the base of the tart: Combine the Almond Meal, shredded coconut, and egg in the bowl of a food processor and process until smooth. Press into the pie tin and bake for 15 minutes until it becomes golden brown. Remove from oven and let cool. Set aside.
3. In a large saucepan, liquefy the coconut oil over a medium flame and add the remainder of the ingredients. Stir until smooth and pour into the cooled pie crust. Store in the refrigerator for 2 hours or until set. Slice into 8 pieces and serve, or store in a container for up to a week in the fridge.

Nutritional Facts: Cal: 219; Carb: 5.5g; Protein: 3.5g; Fat: 15g; Fiber: 1.5g; Sugars: 1g; Cholesterol: 16mg; Sodium: 50mg

15 10-WEEK MEAL PLAN

Week 1

Day	Breakfast	Lunch	Dinner
Day 1	Italian Ham Biscuits	Shirataki Spinach Noodles	Salmon Salad Rolls
Day 2	Bacon, Cheese and Chive Scones	Cheesy Pesto Pasta Bowl	Leftover Salad Rolls
Day 3	Italian Ham Biscuits	Steak Salad Cups	Leftover Pesto Pasta Bowls
Day 4	Bacon Cheese and Chive Scones	Avocado Baked Eggs	Zucchini Spiral Salad
Day 5	Italian Ham Biscuits	Curried Shrimp	Leftover Curried Shrimp
Day 6	Bacon, Cheese and Chive Scones	Feta Turkey Patties	Mushroom Burgers
Day 7	Italian Ham Biscuits	Mozzarella in Meatballs	Egg Drop Soup

Week 2

Day	Breakfast	Lunch	Dinner
Day 1	Quick and Easy Keto Breakfast	Filipino Pork Soup	Vegetarian Fajitas
Day 2	Garden Hash	Chimichurri Steak Sandwich	Leftover Pork Soup
Day 3	Green Eggs	Pasta Free Lasagna	Keto Sausages and Peppers
Day 4	Quick and Easy Keto Breakfast	Leftover Lasagna	Southern Shrimp Salad
Day 5	Buttered Herb Eggs	Salmon and Vegetable Noodles	Pulled Pork Pasta
Day 6	Garden Hash	Leftover Pulled Pork Pasta	Leftover Salmon and Vegetable Noodles
Day 7	Sea Skipper's Eggs	Finnan Haddie Fish Burgers	Chicken Pesto Pasta

Week 3

Day	Breakfast	Lunch	Dinner
Day 1	Pumpkin Spiced Overnight Breakfast Oats	Unconventional Beef Curry	Crispy Pork with Zesty Cauliflower Rice
Day 2	Buffalo Chicken Breakfast Cups	Leftover Pork and Cauliflower Rice	Leftover Beef Curry
Day 3	Pumpkin Spiced Overnight Breakfast Oats	Southwestern Cabbage and Bacon	Egg Roll in a Bowl
Day 4	Buffalo Chicken Breakfast Cups	Cod with Mustard Cream Sauce	Creamy Mushroom Chicken
Day 5	Pumpkin Spiced Overnight Breakfast Oats	Leftover Egg Roll in a Bowl	Leftover Cod with Mustard Cream Sauce
Day 6	Buffalo Chicken Breakfast Cups	Leftover Cabbage and Bacon	Leftover Creamy Mushroom Chicken
Day 7	Pumpkin Spiced Overnight Breakfast Oats	Scallops in the Sea	Zucchini au Gratin

Week 4

Day	Breakfast	Lunch	Dinner
Day 1	Chocolate Coconut Granola	Greek Salad	Chicken Laksa
Day 2	Pesto Egg Muffins	Zucchini and Spinach Chowder	Garlic Baked Pork Chops
Day 3	Chocolate Coconut Granola	Salmon and Sautéed Kale	Autumnal Chicken Thighs
Day 4	Pesto Egg Muffins	Buffalo Blue Cheese Burgers	Fisherman's Stew
Day 5	Chocolate Coconut Granola	Leftover Buffalo Burgers	Leftover Chicken Thighs
Day 6	Pesto Egg Muffins	Leftover Pork Chops	Leftover Salmon and Kale
Day 7	Chocolate Coconut Granola	Leftover Chowder	Leftover Fisherman's Stew

Week 5

Day	Breakfast	Lunch	Dinner
Day 1	Tomatillo Keto Muffins	Cream of Mushroom Soup	Vegetarian Fajitas
Day 2	Nutty Baked Brie	Pork with Kale	Leftover Cream of Mushroom Soup
Day 3	Tomatillo Keto Muffins	Leftover Fajitas	Zucchini Pasta and Meatballs
Day 4	Nutty Baked Brie	Leftover Pork with Kale	Leftover Pasta and Meatballs
Day 5	Tomatillo Keto Muffins	Turkey Bacon Meatloaf	Salmon and Kale
Day 6	Nutty Baked Brie	Leftover Meatloaf	Leftover Salmon and Kale
Day 7	Tomatillo Keto Muffins	Scallops in the Sea	Leftover Meatloaf

Week 6

Day	Breakfast	Lunch	Dinner
Day 1	Sea Skipper's Eggs	Quick Pantry Salad	Pasta-Free Lasagna Casserole
Day 2	Garden Hash	Leftover Lasagna	Steak Salad Cups
Day 3	Sea Skipper's Eggs	Curried Shrimp	Glazed Salmon and Noodles
Day 4	Garden Hash	California Tuna Lettuce Wraps	Cauliflower Spanakorizo
Day 5	Sea Skipper's Eggs	Finnan Haddie Fish Burgers	Pulled Pork Pasta
Day 6	Garden Hash	Leftover Pulled Pork	Leftover Curried Shrimp
Day 7	Sea Skipper's Eggs	Leftover Finnan Haddie	Leftover Cauliflower

Week 7

Day	Breakfast	Lunch	Dinner
Day 1	Italian Ham Biscuits	Slow-Cooked Barbecue Beef	Southern Shrimp Salad
Day 2	Bacon, Cheese and Chive Scones	Chimichurri Steak Sandwiches	Seafood Vegetable Stir-Fry
Day 3	Italian Ham Biscuits	Leftover Barbecue Beef	Leftover Steak Sandwiches
Day 4	Bacon Cheese and Chive Scones	Leftover Shrimp Salad	Leftover Seafood Vegetable Stir-Fry
Day 5	Italian Ham Biscuits	Mediterranean Pulled Pork	Egg Drop Soup
Day 6	Bacon, Cheese and Chive Scones	Leftover Egg Drop Soup	Roasted Provencal Turkey
Day 7	Italian Ham Biscuits	Leftover Turkey	Scallops in the Sea

Week 8

Day	Breakfast	Lunch	Dinner
Day 1	Chocolate Coconut Granola	Turkey Bacon Meatloaf	Bacon Basted Chicken Thighs
Day 2	Pesto Egg Muffins	Leftover Meatloaf	Leftover Chicken Thighs
Day 3	Chocolate Coconut Granola	Keto Sausages and Peppers	Southwestern Cabbage and Bacon
Day 4	Pesto Egg Muffins	Pulled Pork Pasta	Coconut Chicken Curry Soup
Day 5	Chocolate Coconut Granola	Leftover Sausages and Peppers	Leftover Chicken Curry
Day 6	Pesto Egg Muffins	Leftover Pulled Pork Pasta	Leftover Cabbage and Bacon
Day 7	Chocolate Coconut Granola	Classic Tomato Soup	Spicy Poblano Soup

Week 9

Day	Breakfast	Lunch	Dinner
Day 1	Pumpkin Spiced Overnight Breakfast Oats	Roasted Provencal Turkey	Mediterranean Pulled Pork
Day 2	Buffalo Chicken Breakfast Cups	Leftover Pulled Pork	Leftover Provencal Turkey
Day 3	Pumpkin Spiced Overnight Breakfast Oats	Artichoke Chicken Wrapped in Bacon	Salmon Curry
Day 4	Buffalo Chicken Breakfast Cups	Fisherman's Stew	Leftover Turkey
Day 5	Pumpkin Spiced Overnight Breakfast Oats	Leftover Pulled Pork	Leftover Fisherman's Stew
Day 6	Buffalo Chicken Breakfast Cups	Leftover Artichoke Chicken	Leftover Salmon Curry
Day 7	Pumpkin Spiced Overnight Breakfast Oats	Curried Shrimp	Salmon and Sautéed Kale

Week 10

Day	Breakfast	Lunch	Dinner
Day 1	Quick and Easy Keto Breakfast	Cod with Mustard Cream Sauce	Zucchini Pasta and Meatballs
Day 2	Garden Hash	Pasta-Free Lasagna Casserole	Leftover Cod with Mustard Cream Sauce
Day 3	Green Eggs	Leftover Pasta and Meatballs	Thai Chicken Satay and Rice
Day 4	Quick and Easy Keto Breakfast	Pork with Kale	Leftover Lasagna Casserole
Day 5	Buttered Herb Eggs	Leftover Thai Chicken Satay	Egg Roll In a Bowl
Day 6	Garden Hash	Shirataki Spinach Noodles	Leftover Pork with Kale
Day 7	Sea Skipper's Eggs	Salmon and Sautéed Kale	Glazed Salmon and Noodles

16 APPENDIX

To Convert to Metric

Unit	Multiply By	Result
Teaspoons	4.93	Milliliters
Tablespoons	14.79	
Fluid Ounces	29.57	
Cups	236.59	
Pints	473.18	
Quarts	946.36	
Cups	0.236	Liters
Pints	0.473	
Quarts	0.946	
Gallons	3.785	
Ounces	28.35	Grams
Pounds	0.454	Kilograms
Inches	2.54	Centimeters
Fahrenheit	Subtract 32, times 5, divided by 9	Celsius

To Convert from Metric

Unit	Divide By	To Get
Milliliters	4.93	Teaspoons
	14.79	Tablespoons
	29.57	Fluid Ounces
	236.59	Cups
	473.18	Pints
	946.36	Quarts
Liters	0.236	Cups
	0.473	Pints
	0.946	Quarts
	3.785	Gallons
Grams	28.35	Ounces
Kilograms	.454	Pounds
Centimeters	2.54	Inches
Celsius	Multiply by 9, Divide by 5, add 32	Fahrenheit

17 CONCLUSION

Adherence to the Keto Diet to achieve your weight loss goals is achievable if you are able to inject a lot of variety into your diet. With the recipes from these pages, you are able to take better control of your diet. Some recipes here are make ahead so you would be able to do a lot of Prep work for the week ahead, and you can feel free to mix and match recipes to suit your tastes, cravings and most importantly, budget. You can also make adjustments for your snacks and sides should you choose to, provided you are able to maintain your dietary requirements recommended by a nutritionist and your physician.

Do not forget to seek medical clearance before you embark on this diet, and do not forget to check if you are allergic to certain ingredients in these recipes. You may make substitutions as you wish provided they adhere to the recommended ingredients provided for in Chapter 1 of this book. With several recipes in your repertoire, you can now take better control of your diet and embark on your very own weight loss journey.

BONUS: Scanning the following QR code will take you to a web page where you can access 12 fantastic bonuses after leaving your email and an honest review of my book on Amazon: 8 online courses about keto diet and recipes and 4 mobile apps about keto diet and recipes.

Link: https://dl.bookfunnel.com/rb36zmsn6c

Printed in Great Britain
by Amazon

22694968R00053